Get away from me with those Christmas Gifts

This book is for my friends,

particularly David Sheps,

in memory of his mother, Janet Thom Sheps,

who first contributed to and

laughed over the Christmas presents

Get away from me with those Christmas Gifts

AND OTHER REACTIONS

BY *Sylvia Wright*

Illustrations by Sheila Greenwald

McGRAW-HILL BOOK COMPANY, INC.

New York   Toronto   London

The author wishes to thank the following: The MacDowell Colony, for a month of perfect working conditions; Nana and Marcia Robbins, for corroborating the existence and habits of beings such as mumblebees and cattalomes; and, most heartily, Pearl Kazin, without whom pronouns would have had peculiar antecedents, modifiers would have dangled, and situations that should have been chaotic might have been inchoate.

Grateful acknowledgment is also made to the following magazines for permission to include material that first appeared, in somewhat different form, in their pages: Harper's magazine, for "Whose World? and Welcome to It," "Who the Hell Is Holy, Fair, and Wise?" "Get Away from Me with Those Christmas Gifts," "How to Make Chicken Liver Pâté Once," "My Kitchen Hates Me," "Dear Fiduciary Trust Company," "The Death of Lady Mondegreen," "What Was Good Enough for Mr. Rochester," "Quit It, Ompremitywise," and "Picking Your Mate with a Menu"; Vogue, for "What Have I Been Doing All This Time?" "The Fleers of Backford English," and "How to Avoid Emotional Maturity"; The Atlantic Monthly, for "How I Am Never Going to Make Clam Chowder Again"; Harper's Bazaar, for "On Being a Little Bit Sick" and "How to Mend a Broken Heart"; High Fidelity, for "Soap and the Opera"; and Mademoiselle, for "How to Be Happy Though Fired."

GET AWAY FROM ME WITH THOSE CHRISTMAS GIFTS

Library of Congress Catalog Card Number: 57–12597

FIRST EDITION

FOREWORD: *Author? Author?*

THE PUBLISHER wanted this book to have a central theme. Why don't you, he said, be a bachelor girl living alone in New York?

I am, and I tried, and I couldn't. From this, only one conclusion could be drawn. I wasn't. Nowadays, to be something you have to take an attitude, and I couldn't figure out what the attitude was, though I had a hunch it smacked of being a gay, mad gal. I looked up bachelor in the dictionary, and I found that a bachelor, among other things, was a North American fresh-water fish, found chiefly in the Great Lakes regions and southward through the Mississippi, otherwise known as a crappie. So where was I?

The publisher was brave and said, All right, I could let the book creep up on me. Now that it has, I should be able to tell him what it is and who crept up with it.

I can't. There seems to be someone here because the pages are sprinkled with I's, but whoever is here (if anyone) is a different I from me.

All I can tell you is what she did. First, she tried to find out who she was. She thought she could do so by pouncing, so she pounced on her sex, on her name, and on how she spent my time.

This got her nowhere, so she gave up and went wandering around the house, picking things up after herself and putting them down. She wandered into the kitchen and did a little cooking, but presently she threw the cookbook on the floor and went out again. Occasionally she muttered things like Get away, Keep your distance, Who do you think you are? I found this surprising because I think that normally she has a sweet disposition and knows better than to take things out on inanimate objects.

Next she strayed into the library, where she pulled all the books down from the shelves and dipped into them. She wasn't selective: she was just as likely to pull down a corporation report as a book of ballads. Then she tore pages out of them, and mixed them up into a lot of little messes.

Having messed up the library, she went outdoors and began jumping at the world, evidently thinking that whatever was going on was particularly directed at her. Considering how meek I tend to be, I am constantly surprised at how brisk and positive she sounds.

Finally she sat down and wrote a fable. While she was writing, she wouldn't speak to me, but when she had finished, she said in surprise, How did this happen? This must be for you. Then she lost all interest.

So, judging from her behavior, she is perverse, variable, and undefinable. I would think her product would turn out to be likewise but whether it did or not is unimportant, because the minute the publisher got his hands on it, he knew exactly what it was.

This, he said to my surprise, is a book called *Get Away from Me with Those Christmas Gifts.*

S. W.

CONTENTS

IV. JUMPING AT THE WORLD

V. HOW DID THIS HAPPEN?

I

Who's Here, If Anyone?

Whose World? — And Welcome to It

A GOOD MANY PEOPLE, AND SEXUAL AN-thropologists, feel that I, American Woman, am in a state of disarray: I am disturbed about my lot, restless, anxious, confused; insecure, dissatisfied, demanding; lonely, touchy, grouchy; neurotic, psychosomatic, and sexually ambiguous.

Funnily enough, I am also taking over. I am turning the United States into a matriarchy, by which they mean a matriarchate.

They view this with alarm, and so do I. I view with alarm having to be American Woman. Every time I find that I am it, lassitude creeps over me. I would call it boredom, if I didn't know that I shouldn't be bored at being American Woman.

Like all persons, including men, I read the things about American Woman because I think they are going to be about sex. Occasionally they are—bland sex. But the burden is all the ways in which I am found wanting and all the things I should be, do, or make.

Like all women and other precision instruments, I am sensitive and responsive: I weep with delight when they give me a smile and tremble with fear at their frown. So I try. But if this keeps up I will have so many things to be and do that I will never have a moment to myself to find out who's here, if anyone.

3

So I would like to reassure everyone that I am really quite all right. Into each life, a little rain, etc., and sometimes I get caught in it without an umbrella. Try as I will, I always feel that I, person, not I, American Woman, am the one who is drenched. This may be base expediency on my part. Person can dry out. It would take Woman forever.

To start with, I have not taken over. Only a casual look is needed to show that this is not a woman's world.

How can it be, with fluorescent lights in it? I arrive for lunch with a charming man, soignée and smiling elusively. For the moment I am Marlene Dietrich, which is silly because I know I should be trying to be Helpmate. But I figure that that can come later. Everything is fine, and nobody but me knows that I am Marlene Dietrich. Then I go into the ladies' room and look at myself in the mirror under the nice, bright, twentieth-century fluorescent light. Suddenly there in the mirror is Lena the Hyena, on whom "no hoomin" can bear to look.

The last time I went to my doctor's, I was an alert, open-minded American woman, ready to cooperate with the small group of dedicated scientists who are forcing back the frontiers of ignorance. I was only going for a checkup. As I went into the dressing room, I was Ingrid Bergman in a white coat.

Another thing I don't like about fluorescent lights is the sneaky way they wait a while before turning on.

When they did, I knew why I had come. I was sick, fatally sick. I had got to the doctor's just in time.

There is someone behind the mirrors lighted by fluorescent lights who I cannot bear to think is me. Fluorescent lights are to women as Mrs. Mitty is to Walter.

The people who make things to sit on have no consideration for my contours or my *savoir-faire*. In those hammock chairs I have to get into the knee-chest position. Modern upholstered chairs are too long for me from hip to knee. Either I have my legs straight out in front like a doll, or I sit on one foot, which goes to sleep.

Studio couches are another trap. I lean back, happily ready to be the life of the party. Gradually it comes over me that the life of the party is resting on one small bone at the base of my neck, because the studio couch is slowly moving out into the middle of the room.

Architects make the great thick glass doors in new buildings just too heavy for me to push open unless I get into an unattractive position.

People who make keys do something to them that makes them stick when I use them. Men cannot keep their hands off a woman who is struggling with a key. Man takes key. Key has been doctored so that now its works fine. I feel insecure, lonely, grouchy, and mere.

There is a country-wide guild of men in shirt sleeves organized to harry women while parking. One of them always pops up from nowhere, stations himself on the curb, shouts monosyllabic commands, and cramps imaginary wheels. At intervals, he says, "You can make it, lady." I had thought I could, but watching both him and the space makes me anxious. When I finally get parked, and perhaps it did take me a little longer than it should have, he goes off, satisfied that I couldn't have done it without him. The most expert of this group is detailed to make me nervous while getting my car onto a ferryboat.

The other day I bought a bed pillow. Attached to one end was a large tag with cryptic notations about license, certification, Act of Congress, and entirely new material. In large black letters, it said:

5

DO NOT REMOVE THIS TAG
UNDER PENALTY OF THE LAW

It's my pillow, isn't it? I paid for it. Why can't I take off the tag? But I don't. There might be a surprise raid.

Zippers are to convince me that I should learn to keep my butterfingers out of modern technology and recognize the need for experts. In the old days, I could always sew on another hook and eye. Now I'm lucky if I escape with any skin except of my teeth, not to mention an intact dress.

They put the tops of jars on too tight.

Arranging flowers is womanly, and, as all womanly occupations are supposed to be but aren't, rather fun. So they're beginning to take it away. The last time someone sent me flowers, they were stiffly set in a papier-mâché vase, ready for a funeral. A slip came with them announcing that the flowers had been fixed with Floralife powder, which would make them last longer. It said under no circumstances was I (amateur!) to change the water or rearrange the flowers.

Floralife powder looks like sludge. I peeked.

It is true that American Man is also sitting in a hammock chair, under fluorescent lights, facing a three-way mirror, and struggling with a stuck zipper. But look at the difference. Don't ask me why, but it doesn't puncture his ego as it does mine. No one tells him (though I fear they are beginning to) that on his every action depends the manliness of American man. Either he doesn't notice, or he curses.[1] Fearlessly he

---

[1] In the speed and single-mindedness of social advance, certain capacities remain dormant. As yet, we have no tradition of feminine cursing. When American Woman accepts her true role in American life, she may find the time, leisure, and self-confidence necessary to express herself, as men have always done, in those arts and graces which, luxuries in a competitive

rips the tag off the pillow, while talking about something else. He gets the tops off jars. Thus, instinctively, he asserts his primary maleness (presently you'll see where I picked up this nice phrase) and creates an interpersonal relationship in which I respond according to the basic laws of my psychophysical being.

I mean I love him.

The second thing which worries the commentators on American Woman is that I don't know the difference between men and women. Not the obvious difference (come now!) but the difference between his and my role in life. This could be dire, as I realized when I read the issue of *Life* magazine entirely devoted to what one writer therein called that "fascinating, puzzling, eminently noticeable figure"—American Woman. (You can't miss me, possibly because I'm half the population.)

Among the articles was one which contained the conclusions of a number of psychiatrists and psychologists. One of these gentlemen drew a fearsome picture: "The factory couple, leaving perhaps on the same bus in the morning, both perhaps wearing trousers, he soldering the radio parts which she later puts together on an assembly line, coming home equally tired to their frozen-food ready-cooked dinners and the television set they have bought with their joint earnings, are sexually undifferentiated at all times except in the nuptial embrace. The relationship is mutually insulting to their primary maleness and femaleness."

This doesn't appall me as much as it does the writer. I can't help it, but it sounds cozy. There we are, both with our

---

society, are enrichments of a civilized life. Until she can develop herself along this previously purely masculine line, and make it her own, she cannot be said to have accepted her responsibilities as a member of her sex.

legs in trousers up on the coffee table, comfortably tired and looking at television together. Soon we will have a lovely time getting all sexually differentiated.

Nor do I understand why the writer minds the trousers. If it were a Chinese woman going out to help her husband get the water buffalo out of the rice paddy, and returning home equally tired, would he feel that they were insulting each other mutually? A little sexual undifferentiation can be helpful to get one (male or female) through a hard day.

My negative reaction here may throw some doubt on my primary femaleness, but really and truly I do know the differences between men and women. According to my observations, they are as follows:

Women wearing trousers put their hands in the pockets. Men wearing trousers keep things in the pockets.

When a woman sits down on a sofa with little pillows on it, she cuddles into them. When a man does so, he pulls all the pillows out from behind him and throws them to the other end of the sofa.

Women go to the farthest corners of restaurants and sit with their backs to the wall. Men are quite at ease standing up at a bar in the middle of a room.

Before men open cans, they always put them right side up. Women, figuring that it makes no difference, are likely to open them upside down. This is subtly unnerving to men.

A man can go happily along for two or three weeks owing a drink or a lunch to another man. During an equivalent period, a woman who owes another woman a dime will be deeply anxious and disturbed.

Women who have to wear glasses take them off to get a good look at a man. Men who wear glasses keep them on to look at a woman. From this I deduce that women are more interested in being looked at. Men are more interested in looking. Everyone wants to make sure that I realize that men are aggressive and women are passive. From this example everyone can see that I do. Unless it means that women don't really believe they see better with glasses on.

Now that it is clear that I can distinguish between men and women, I would like to go further and say that there are many ways in which I think women are inferior to men. The present situation is an excellent example. The learned professional men who view women with alarm apparently feel in some way squeezed by women. Their reaction is to analyze, to generalize, to formulate explanations, definitions, remedies. Here we see man's basic drive to organize his surroundings, to make laws, to control, even to create.

Women who feel squeezed by men react quite differently. More cautious by the demands of her biological nature, woman instinctively decides not to rock the boat. In such circumstances, woman often says nothing at all. The squeezing might stop.

It is only fair to say that there are some women writers in the group who must feel squeezed by women, too. I think this is a mistake on their part in a world where there are two sexes.

Some women are more restless, anxious, and insecure than men because they can get in trouble in a way that a man can't. I wouldn't call this exactly a biological inferiority. I think it is a biological difference, whose societal implications would bear further analysis, since they are, in essence, a deeply telling comment on society. This one. That's all I seem to be able to deduce about that.

One good reason for all the woman-questioning is that I am a sitting duck. It isn't nice to criticize someone in a minority group. I'm equal now, so I'm not in a minority group. I'm the only group that is equal and a fine big group to criticize.

And here I think we should let bygones be bygones. I didn't ask to be emancipated. That was my great-aunt Melusina.

Now, am I clear about my role today? Yes, I have that straight, too. First, I must be motherly, because, if I am not, I make things difficult for the psychiatrists. This was made clear in the *Life* article referred to above. A Beverly Hills psychiatrist was quoted as saying that it is becoming harder and harder to find examples of simple emotional disorder in the Los Angeles area. Character structure has broken down in Los Angeles, because mothers are being fatherly and fathers are being motherly. "The old-fashioned tyrannical fathers," he said, "produced children who at least had enough character to become neurotic, and these children became neurotic in ways that one could get at and treat. Now people are becoming diffuse and treatment is much more difficult."

I am to be motherly enough to keep my husband fatherly enough to make my children neurotic enough for the psychiatrists to get at.

What else?

Serve delicious, well-rounded, attractive, ample meals, not too ready-cooked. Don't let anyone get fat.

Don't work if married and have children. Work on something or I will be too dependent on children and at a loss when they leave home.

While children are at home, train them in every way possible to cope with difficult world. After children leave home, don't tell them anything I have learned by experience and they haven't. Hold tongue and baby sit.

Don't love son too much: this will make him a homosexual. Don't love him with restraint: this will make him a juvenile delinquent, the little bastard.

Don't have little bastard, even though even a sitting duck may be somebody's mother. If so, give him up for adoption and seek counseling.

Keep home fresh and immaculate. Have home look lived in. Keep everything clean. Don't be compulsive about cleaning.

Use make-up to keep husband's love. Avoid make-up clog. Be gay and spontaneous. Guard against expression lines.

Do good. Do it myself. Vote.

Have I forgotten anything?

Oh, yes, love, that is, love-making. Even if future husband does not want to buy pig in poke, stay in poke until married, owing to societal possibility (emotional connotations of which are deeply disturbing to normal woman) mentioned above. After marriage, do not be pig. Go whole hog. This means, talk it over.

No matter what evidence have to contrary, do not consider love-making normal human instinct. No matter what evidence have to contrary, slightly inept performance cannot be pleasure. Love, an art.

Something else is left out. Be good. This is the one that stumps them nowadays. Under the circumstances, they have worked out a clever formula: if you don't know what being good is, be everything.

Everyone can see that I am fully informed. Does everyone feel better?

There's just one difficulty. Something smells a little stale to me, and I think it is my infinite variety. My unemancipated great-aunt had a diversion which I lack: she could be eccentric. I would like to have one tiny foible. I would like to save string, be scared of the telephone, let my heels run over, not wear gloves. Sometime I would like to make a little scene, while I am still young enough to do it without being described as a naughty old lady. I would like to have one crackpot notion, one little way, or, just once, one of my moods.

It may be my world at that. I just washed it, and I can't do anything with it.

Who the Hell Is Holy, Fair, and Wise?

IT MIGHT BE TRYING TO BE NAMED DI-
nah, or Rose-Marie, or Mariana-in-the-Moated Grange, but
it's torture to be named Sylvia.

Anybody named Sylvia learns at an early age not to wince
when introduced at a party. Either people say, "Who is Silvia?" and beam delightedly at their pinpoint precision with
Shakespeare, or they say, "Sylvia's hair is like the night,"
and, in my case, guffaw, since my hair is not a bit like the
night. (I am a rufous blonde.) I also sit and suffer humorous, meaning looks while some singer moos on about "*L' in-
grate Sylvie*," who has convinced him that the pleasure of
love only lasts for a moment, while the sorrow of love lasts
a lifetime.

Every time an author creates a really terrific heroine—
beautiful, intelligent, distinguished, mysterious—he leaps
on the name Sylvia. Even so down-to-earth a writer as
Upton Sinclair was carried away by the name. His Sylvia was
the belle of her state (state, not town), and "suitors crowded
about her like moths about a candle flame." Yes, that old
muckraker, Upton Sinclair. Here is what seizes him when he
describes her: "I know that a heroine must be slender and
exquisite, must be sensitive and haughty and aristocratic. Sylvia was all this, in truth; but how shall I bring to you the
thrill of wonder that came to me when I encountered her—

13

that living joy she was to me forever after." This is a fine, fruity, aged-in-the-wood example of the Sylvia mystique.

I first became aware of the cross I bear when I was a very small child, playing in a wood in Berkeley, California, in a garment called a "nature suit." This is not what it sounds like, but a one-piece gingham play suit with longish shorts and straps over the shoulders trimmed with rickrack. At the time it was considered advanced, but healthy.

My mother and a strange lady encountered me and my mother introduced me. The strange lady looked misty and said, "Ah, yes, a wood nymph."

I was told this was the meaning of my name, and I promptly became a wood nymph. I enjoyed it enormously, but shortly thereafter for the first time in my life I took a realizing sense of myself in a long mirror. I did not see an ethereal fairylike sprite in flowing pale-green draperies. I saw a small, solemn-looking, tubby, rufous (straight-haired) blonde in a wrinkled nature suit. My yells of rage and disillusionment were heart-rending.

Later on people decided that the perfect book to give me was Lewis Carroll's *Sylvie and Bruno*. I admire Lewis Carroll very much, but Sylvie is second only to Elsie Dinsmore as the most nauseating child in literature. (On second thought, Bruno is worse. Sylvie at least can talk. Bruno says, "Doos oo know?" and "Hurted mine self *welly* much.") Sylvie is described as "one of the sweetest and loveliest little maidens it has ever been my lot to see . . . rosy cheeks and sparkling eyes . . . wealth of curling brown hair [Sylvias always have wealths of hair]." Sylvie is always standing on tiptoe to kiss old people impulsively. She also indulges in the same boring and cheeky logic Alice does (but Alice is not sweet): Bruno says he is busy as the day is long, and Sylvia corrects, "No, no, you're busy as the day is *short!*"

14   *Holy, Fair, and Wise?*

The worst is the lockets. Sylvie is given a choice of two bejeweled ones. One is inscribed, "All will love Sylvie," and the other, "Sylvie will love all." She chooses the second because, "It's very nice to be loved, but it's nicer to love other people." I don't believe I can go on.

Yes, I can. I remember my favorite scene. A boy named Uggug, the incarnation of a horrid child, empties a butter dish on Sylvie. She is noble about it.

Actually *Sylvie and Bruno* is not a children's book. A large part of it is about some equally icky grownups who have long conversations over tea about free will, duty, and syllogisms. I doubt if anybody who gave it to me had read it. I doubt if anyone who is not named Sylvia has read it, except possibly a few Brunos. The aftereffect on them must be frightful.

Another of the traumatic experiences of my childhood was when my school formed a glee club, which I joined as a soprano. Naturally, their first selection, to be sung before the whole assembly, was "Who Is Silvia?". I was thirteen; my class was the youngest in the upper school, and so I stood in the front row.

I knew it was going to be awful and for nights ahead of time I lay awake trying to get sick. There was no escape. When the day arrived, I, dogged, spherical, and bursting with rude health, had to stand there and shrill out, "Holy, fair, and wise is she: The heaven such grace did le-end her." My whole class went into paroxysms of giggles, and by the time love was repairing to my eyes, the glee club was inaudible.

People in Cambridge, Massachusetts, where my grandparents lived, assumed that I was named after a figment of my grandmother's imagination. My grandmother was a novelist; she fell under the sway of the name; and she wrote a novel that had not one, but two Sylvias. She had the inesti-

15

mable grace to create a heroine (the main Sylvia) who was thirty-eight and had snow-white hair (a wealth), and to let her, in the end, win the charming scholarly hero from a younger and more dynamic lady. But she couldn't resist making her "ethereal," "delicate," "transparently pale." They laughed when they asked if I were named for her.

In actual fact my mother irresponsibly named me after a little English girl she had met while traveling. The English girl had a younger sister named Phyllis, and neatly enough, my mother produced a Phyllis about three years after me. Bad as it was to be named Sylvia, it was worse to have Phyllis trailing after you, equally tubby, unspritelike, and not even pastoral-looking.

When we complained, my mother added insult to injury by explaining that in each case she had been somewhat at a loss for a name because she was confidently expecting Benjamin. She said she herself had always suffered because people kept asking her, ha, ha, if she thought she had married the Wright man.

My older brother called me "Saliva."

A little later, my father introduced me to a series of novels by Compton MacKenzie in which the heroine was named Sylvia Scarlett. At this point I gave up, as this is the Sylvia to end all Sylvias. She acts with a Pierrot troupe, runs away from home, gets married and divorced before she is twenty, goes on the stage, travels all over the world, lives in sin, gets mixed up in World War I, has a mystical experience, travels with a troupe of brigands through the war-torn Balkans, and finally cements relations with her true love, a highborn Englishman with a bar sinister, who was once a monk. I was of course supposed to identify myself with this lady and enjoy it, but I was jealous as hell.

Here is how Sylvia Scarlett talks at nineteen: "A man who

admires a woman's intelligence is like a woman who admires her friend's looking glass—each one is granting an audience to himself."

A heroine named, say, Frances could never get away with this sort of thing.

My worst experience was when a friend of mine (named Frances) published a short story in which the heroine was obviously me. People asked me about it warily, as if I had done something a little indecent. I felt a little indecent myself because in the story I was going to bed with somebody I have never met.

My friend had made it perfectly clear the heroine was me. She even called her Sylvia—no bones about it. When I asked her if she didn't think she might have changed the name, she said kindly, "Why, of course, it was based a little on you, but I never thought about the name." Sylvia, she felt, is in the public domain. I can't help feeling that common decency should have made her call the girl Cynthia, at least. Addlepated people often call me that anyway—when they don't call me Phyllis.

To crown this, I was making what I thought was a funny, teeth-in-the-wind anecdote about this for some friends when an ethereal, delicate girl (named Nancy) looked me over and said with detachment, "As it happens, the heroine of the novel I'm writing is named Sylvia."

She needn't have looked at me like that. I know I don't look like her heroine.

Lately heroines have been getting less romantic, and I began to hope Sylvia would just fade away. Then I had a shock. The name is so generic it's going on in another guise. What I'm now beginning to find, particularly in women's magazines, is this sort of thing: "A charming, personable young woman I'll call Sylvia B. was referred to me because of severe

17

headaches. A change of glasses, treatment for sinusitis, and the usual anodynes had been of no help. She had been subjected to spinal tap, complete blood count, brainwave test, urinalysis, skull X-rays and intensive eye examinations, basal metabolism test, and a lengthy hospitalization." In addition, the writer goes on to say, she didn't like her children, was unenthusiastic about sex relations with her husband, fought with her mother-in-law, and had no friends. Want to know what was wrong with her? She was too neat.

I found the following item in the *Wall Street Journal*. "Christmas bonuses on Wall Street will be relatively slim or non-existent. 'When we probably won't pay a bonus to Sylvia, you know how things are,' says a broker. Sylvia is the firm's girl Friday—the head bookkeeper, scourge of the clerks, chief worrier and No. 1 on any list of beneficences."

There's your modern heroine, the new Sylvia, and I don't like her any better than the other. She may become an even greater source of embarrassment. For a whole month, a large, shiny, famous woman's magazine was on the front of all the newsstands with a gleaming headline announcing, "Sylvia Is Frigid."

If I ever write a novel and manage to stop myself from calling all the horrid characters Frances and Nancy, I will still try not to call the heroine Sylvia. But the compulsion may become too great, and if it does, Sylvia of course will be slender, exquisite, sensitive, haughty, aristocratic, ethereal, holy, fair, and wise. This is enough to make anyone frigid. It will, of course, be a modern novel, so I am working on the man who will conquer this unfortunate condition. He is wonderful. He is tall, poised, sensitive, manly, haughty, aristocratic, holy, dark, and wise. I deserve him.

What Have I Been Doing All This Time?

IF YOU HAVE NEVER, WHILE READING (ON A suburban train, say, every wicker seat filled by a man who might always have been there, he inexorably growing gray and paunchy in forever the same position, crowded in conning folded long (in fours) the same inevitable newspaper) the life story or interview with or take on some person suddenly now successful, with some production the cause: a book published, a deal consummated, a performance hailed; found then your mind, utterly without either direction or intention, methodically noting the date of the first production, book, deal, or performance; then placing below it the year of birth, already only by subtraction from that one that presently is the one you are writing in the upper right-hand corner of your checks acquired, then again subtracting, to come finally to the discovery of the leaden nugget of information that he (or she) was at that time ten years younger then you (unutterably condemned to indistinction) are at this moment; then you need not with this article go on, proceed, or even (any further word for that matter) continue.

But if you do in this weakness find yourself trapped or entrenched (and if you must know, he—inexorably, in Oxford, Mississippi, remaining being, and that not so surprisingly, but still trenchantly, himself (of this, enough!)—was twenty-seven when his first book was printed), read on.

19

William Faulkner is not as disheartening as some, like the eighteen-year-olds. I'll kill them. But I am older than twenty-seven, and I haven't had a book published before. I haven't swum the English Channel. What have I been *doing* all this time?

In his youth, Faulkner once said, he spent some time in "undirected and uncorrelated reading." Could this explain my wasted youth? My own reading was as directed and correlated as a bulldozer. I read *The Little Colonel*. Then I read *The Little Colonel's House Party*. Then I read *The Little Colonel's Holidays*, *The Little Colonel's Hero*, *The Little Colonel at Boarding School*, and so on down to *The Little Colonel's Knight Comes Riding*. I read *Patty Fairfield*. Then I read *Patty in the City*, *Patty in Paris*. . . . Please don't write and tell me which ones I've left out. There are fourteen Little Colonels and I don't know how many Patty Fairfields, and I am not being paid by the word.

There are going to be howls of outrage, but I'll say it: reading all the Little Colonels is a waste of time. You can get the good red meat (only it isn't, it's bu'ful 'trawberries an' cream) by reading one. More is self-indulgence.

Faulkner might have read one Little Colonel—there are colonels in his background—but after that I'm sure he skipped uncorrelatedly to *The Decline of the West*. Now I think of it, this may explain Faulkner. Anyone who wants really to waste time may explore this theory for a Ph. D. thesis: Two Little Knights of Kentucky: Prototypes for Uncle Gavin?

I'm sure Faulkner never had to play field hockey. He didn't spend ten of the most formative autumns of his life buckled into shin guards, panting up and down hockey fields.

Field hockey is total waste because adult life provides no opportunity to use its chief skill, which consists in hitting other women on the shins with a wooden stick.

There is also shorthand, which I studied hard. Though when called upon I never could read it, my shorthand became so ingrained that I walked around town tracing signs in shorthand with my right forefinger. Even today, when I never use shorthand, I can't stop myself from doing this. Every time I pass Schrafft's, I have to do the shorthand symbol. You should see me doing First National City Bank of New York, and "Wash your clothes with Surf and they'll smell like sunshine." This sort of activity distracts one from more uncorrelated thoughts.

When I was released by the educational authorities, I discovered that the tendency painfully to acquire useless knowledge had become a habit. I promptly learned all the leitmotifs in the Wagner operas. I can hum "The Renunciation of Love," or "Hagen's Perfidious Friendship" at the drop of a Tarnhelm. I might say I have also spent time trying to figure out how many bodies, and when, were in the grave in *Intruder in the Dust*. I'm still working on this. I think there is a mistake.

I have now realized that I am too old to begin again, become uncorrelated, and get somewhere. I have come to the conclusion that the only salvation is to learn to waste time in the most complicated and difficult way possible. This makes you feel better. Take each day as it comes, and, at its close, say to yourself, "Today I wasted time as well as I could. Tomorrow I'll do it better." Gradually your life will be informed with new purpose.

This mechanism, offered here for the first time to the troubled citizens of the Atomic Age, and which I haven't been able to make up my mind whether to call compulsive sloth or creative inertia, may well save more people from expensive sojourns in mental hospitals than any other single finding, including finding no money.

Among artists compulsive sloth has long been known. Painters have a built-in device: They clean brushes. Musicians are perhaps less well equipped: there is not much they can do except rearrange their music and talk on the telephone. Writers, of all artists, are the most inventive. (I have to stop for a moment and mend my pencil sharpener. A piece just broke off, and it means a complicated gluing job. I may have to go out and buy some special glue. This pencil sharpener cost ten cents, but it was a good one. Waste not, want not.)

Women writers clean. For example, they may carve the dirt out of the cracks in the floor with a bobby pin, or read the fine print on the Bab-O can. Brass is excellent: If you want to get the brass polished, invite a writer who is working hard on an article to come and stay with you. A device I particularly enjoy is cleaning the dirt out of all the o's, e's, a's, etc., on the typewriter with a pin.

But with a little time and thought you can be much more inventive. I admire a writer I know who has a tin tray which he sprays with plastic paint. He always has to go out and buy a new color because he doesn't like the one he's used before. Another writer cleans up his yard. He collects all the twigs, breaks them into exactly even lengths, and fits them into large facial-tissue boxes, saved for the purpose. Packed with twigs, the boxes are used as kindling in the fireplace. Unfortunately, the supply is greater than the demand. At last report he had eighty-two tissue boxes filled

What Have I Been Doing?

with twigs stacked in his cellar. The corners of the boxes are carefully squared.

I have a writer friend whose apartment is so immaculate that she is hard put to it to be compulsively slothful. But she manages it. The other day, I found her contemplating a vase containing, as a winter decoration, branches of black alder, covered with small red berries. The berries had begun to shrivel a little, and were not as bright as formerly. "I'm wondering," she said dreamily, "if they'd look better if I touched up each berry with a little red nail polish."

People who do not face up to things often call their compulsive sloth their hobby. This is prevalent among New Englanders, who are so rock-ribbed that they do not face up to having any kind of sloth. One must, however, give New Englanders credit for the evolution of an excellent device, under the guise of a hobby. This is genealogy. By its nature, work on it can go on almost indefinitely (depending on how you feel about Adam and Eve), and the equipment, blank books with holes in them through which you poke your ancestors further and further into the dark backward of time, is peculiarly, even ecstatically, satisfying.

Another advantage to calling your compulsive sloth a hobby is that, if it becomes extensive enough, you can be an authority. A New Englander, with whom I have a generic genealogical connection (he's my brother) has by this method become an authority—perhaps the authority—on the records of figure-skating competitions. One of his friends collects the numbers on obsolete railroad engines.

Do not think for a moment that it is only unusual people like writers and New Englanders who can be compulsively slothful. I know a simple housewife, with two small children, who does all her own work, who has created one of the most brilliant forms of compulsive sloth I know, since, in addition to being slothful, it makes all the other mothers in the neighborhood feel inferior. While she is making an adult-sized apple pie for her family, she makes small apple pies for her children and any neighborhood children who wander in. She makes them in the caps of Coca-Cola bottles. First she digs the cork out of the bottle caps. Then she makes little circles of dough, which she cuts out with the gadget for making watermelon balls. She cuts up little bits of apple, dots them with tiny bits of butter, sugar, and cinnamon, and puts on a little tiny top crust, which she pierces with a pin.

To rest up, my friend reads *The Letters of D. H. Lawrence*. She reads them over and over again, because they are restful. When Lawrence felt burned out, she tells me, he went into the kitchen and made marmalade. Probably he had no bottle caps.

If you become really experienced, you can indulge in snowballing or concentric compulsive sloth. The easiest way to begin is to straighten things. You must throw away the pile of newspapers. But there was an advertisement you meant to cut out, and you always mean to read the News of the Week in Review. So you have to go through them. While looking for your ad, you come upon one for soap flakes. Maybe soap flakes should be added to your shopping list. You go into the kitchen to see how much soap flakes is left. Just enough to wash that blouse. You get out the blouse, but it has a button off. You get out your sewing basket, which needs to be straightened out, if you're to find a button. This means winding all the loose thread back around the spools and securing it in those little slots. While doing this, you turn up a small sample of material which you were planning to use for a slip cover for your couch.

You take it out, and put it on the end of the couch to study the effect. While studying the effect, you realize it would be better if the room weren't so messy. You must throw away that pile of newspapers. But first you have to look through them.

This is a simplified example. If you work on it, you can snowball compulsive sloth into a whole day's waste.

Everything seems to be immaculate. Shall I sift the ashes in the fireplace? Paint my old trunk blue? Rearrange the books according to the age of the author when first published? I'm on the verge of having to do something uncorrelated, which might turn out to be constructive.

II

Wandering Around the House

Get Away from Me with Those Christmas Gifts

I DON'T WANT TO THROW A MONKEY
wrench—even a hand-crafted personalized monkey wrench
you can plant ivy in—into the works and grace of the holiday
season, but there are certain things that if anyone gives them
to me for Christmas I will scream. I will not scream from
rage, but because I will be losing my grip on reality. Has anyone but me been really reading the catalogues and the gift
(never "present") sections of the magazines? Or has it been
building up so slowly that no one has noticed?

Something phrenetic, sinister, and crazed is going on in
the gift world.

In case someone should think I am the one who's crazed,
I will list the things in the gift line I am prepared to put
up with. I don't want them, but I won't fly off the handle if
I get them. When you read my list, you'll see how reasonable
I am, and will, I hope, be convinced that I haven't made it
up about the other objects—the ones that are out to get me.

For example, I accept ivy—and the fact that it can be
planted in anything: a cup and saucer, a coffee grinder, a bird
cage, a cranberry picker, a spoon rack. Ivy has a reason for
being—to take up the Americana slack. An Americana item
such as a cobbler's bench or an ox yoke which is of no use to
anyone can be an ivy planter.

I accept dispensers. Dispensers are things it is more complicated to put the thing into than to leave it where it is. But dispensers are a part of our national life. Americans are the original canister kids: we love to waste time taking the coffee out of the perfectly good can it came in and putting it into another can which matches the one the flour is in. We like to send in coupons and get a hand-painted can to put the can of scouring powder in so it won't look like a can of scouring powder. The powder has to go through two sets of holes and soon the whole thing is clogged up. But dispensers are here to stay.

As gifts, dispensers usually contain Scotch tape or stamps, and they are sometimes made in fourteen-carat gold to give the woman who already has everything (including an identical brass Scotch-tape dispenser from last Christmas).

Incidentally, the woman who has everything has gone so far that all you can give her now is something vulgar.

There are two ideas I find irritating, but which I will tolerate. One is that everyone in this country has melted butter with everything, and that every household must have a quantity of individualized small pipkins, piggins, firkins, and noggins to serve it in. The other is that everyone likes to eat off what we used to call skewers, and what are now, for some reason, called kabobs. One can always use the kabobs for what one used to use skewers for, to truss a chicken.

I will go along with the fact that, as a nation, we can't leave the telephone alone at Christmastime. I anticipate a plastic cover in a decorator color (any color except tan, which is always called "natural"). There may be a lamp to go on top of it and a secretary to go underneath (a secretary is something you write on). This is a magnetic age, so the secretary will be magnetized, and will grip a magnetic pencil. Once I get the pencil loose, I lose it as easily as any other, but I'm not fussing. I like things that stick to things, and I'm waiting for the time when the telephone gets a magnetized base and can be attached to the family bulletin board. These days, family bulletin boards are trying to achieve togetherness with anything they can get.

I accept the fact that television has given the gift manufacturers a shot in the arm. At present, they are still getting rid of the hassocks the college girls wouldn't buy, under the name of television viewers. Soon, television and ivy will meet —but let's cross that bridge when we come to it.

I'm not even complaining about the axiom gifts—those eight balls, and jiggers made in the shape of thimbles, so that you can pour someone "just a thimbleful." I've puzzled over how they originate and decided that, quite by accident, someone says to a gift manufacturer, "Little pitchers have big ears," and the manufacturer quickly makes a little china pitcher with two great big china ears. Because it is so small that it won't hold anything, it's either called a collector's item or a conversation piece.

I had better explain the fine distinction here. A conversation piece is similar to a collector's item, but it is a little more transient, sophisticated, and likely to have to do with drinking. Pink-elephant beer mugs and Diamond Jim apron waistcoats are conversation pieces. Salt and pepper shakers made in the shapes of Laurel and Hardy, and miniature mustache cups, 1⅜ inches in diameter, are collector's items. A third category, when the copy writer doesn't wish to be so heavy-handed, is described as "comment-provoking." This includes tired glasses, made to sag on one side, in which you,

you joker, are supposed to serve the fourth round, and plastic ice cubes with realistic bugs frozen in them.

I will accept (just barely) that white head, called Paddy O'Hair, which sprouts green grass for hair and eyebrows.

I will accept even supererogatory gifts, by which I mean bath mats with footprints on them.

As you can see, I'm reasonable. Calm. Quite calm. I won't make trouble. But there comes a point—

Take the gifts that complicate.

There's a tape measure with a battery light for measuring in closets. I can't figure out what it is I should be measuring in a closet. It could be the closet itself, but why have I got the door closed?

There's a gadget to be plugged into the cigarette lighter of your car in which you can roast two frankfurters in their own juices in seven minutes. Presumably you've been driving along an American highway, and you can get a frankfurter at least once every mile, and you can get it in a roll, with mustard, a napkin, and possibly even on a plate. You receive the hot-dog sizzler for Christmas and where are you? Shut up in the front seat with mustard all over everything, napkins blowing out the window, and rolls on the floor. And next year, you'll have to turn it in for the new sizzler which splits its own rolls, and has a squeezable plastic mustard dispenser attached.

But these are mild compared with the gift which is "double-purpose" or "two-in-one."

There's the double-purpose coffee-mill lamp. It is a lamp for a bedside table on top of a real coffee grinder. Either you take the coffee beans into the bedroom to grind your breakfast coffee or you unplug the lamp and take it into the kitchen. Or you sleep in the kitchen.

There's another lamp which is a china pig bank. There's no way to get out the money without breaking the lamp.

There are red and green port and starboard lanterns, which are also whisky decanters. When you're not pouring out of them, you put them on the port and starboard ends of the mantelpiece. Then you spend the rest of the winter trying to figure out which way your mantelpiece is sailing.

There's the folding hanger with the clothes brush on the end. If I had one folding hanger with a clothes brush on the end, where in all the wide world would it be when I wanted to brush my suit? Holding up my winter coat. How can I bear to have all folding hangers with clothes brushes on the ends, but what other solution is there?

There's that bell which really rings which is a Martini mixer. Do I want my Martinis wired for sound, and if I do, how can I stop myself from experimenting until I find out how far I can ring the bell without spilling the Martinis?

The double-purpose device has crept into gifts for children. Any toy or piece of children's equipment can be made double-purpose by attaching a music box. The theory is that the music soothes the child into behaving like an angel. The musical toothbrush holder, for example, plays a gay tune when the brush is removed. This, they say, will encourage Junior to brush his teeth. In my opinion it will encourage Junior to remove the brush, put it back again, remove the brush, put it back again, remove—

Another is the bed lamp with music box. It has a shade that tilts, and when you tilt it the light turns on. At some point, it plays a tune which will "make children want to go to sleep." What child worth his salt would go to sleep when he could be tilting a shade back and forth to make a light go on?

33

Double-purpose doesn't stop with double. Take ivy in a cobbler's bench. Soon you have ivy in a cobbler's bench with a lamp attached. Then you have ivy in a cobbler's bench with a lamp and a place for a highball glass. Ash trays. Pencil sharpeners.

It's the same with dispensers. Scotch-tape dispensers get paper-clip trays on top. Then they have paper-clip trays and places to put ball-point pens. Then the pen is a ball-point dachshund.

This is the malignant gift.

There's a classic example. Some years ago, someone dredged up some otherwise useless odds and ends of Plexiglas, sharpened one edge of each piece, and sold them as windshield de-icers. This is all right—in fact it's American ingenuity. Next Christmas there were some left over, so he put initials on them and sold them (for a little more) as personalized windshield de-icers. Well, you wouldn't want your windshield de-icer to get mixed up with someone else's. The following Christmas he bored holes in them, stuck in little chains, and brought out personalized windshield de-icer key rings. You won't believe me if you haven't been following closely, but at present we are at the stage of the personalized windshield de-icer key ring with miniature compass.

A normally adjusted American ought to be able to turn on the ignition, whip out the key, jump out of the car, de-ice the windshield, and use the compass to track his way back to the driver's seat. If it were night, he might need a flashlight to see the compass, which will give you an idea of what he will get next.

But next after that they will attach a hot-dog sizzler. Or a music box. . . .

I can't go it. They're overestimating my emotional stability.

A year or so ago, someone brought out a realistic-looking set of false teeth (politely called dentures) which you wound with a key and which went yakity-yakity-yakity. Next year, they elaborated. They produced the denture bottle opener. It fastened to the wall and came complete with three gum-colored wall screws. "Ridiculous, gruesome, and fun! They're so real-looking that Grandpa will snap his teeth just to be sure he's got them." Next? A death's-head bottle opener which glowed in the dark so you could open beer bottles while watching television. See how it's building up? See what is coming? This year, while the television rages on, those teeth will be going yakity-yakity-yakity, glowing in the dark, and snapping off bottle caps. And grass will be growing out of them.

How to Make Chicken Liver Pâté Once

Judging from the women's maga-
zines, one of life's great experiences is when someone says,
"This is simply delicious. Do tell me how you make it."
Beaming, the hostess promptly replies, indented:

> Take a level cup of flour. Add one medium egg, lightly
> beaten, a scant tablespoonful of grated Parmesan cheese,
> etc., etc.

and a complete recipe follows, down to

> This serves six.

What I don't understand is how these ladies start from
absolute scratch. They never have dabs in their iceboxes.
They never put the leftover string beans into the macaroni
and cheese, to get rid of them and see what it would be like.
They just make macaroni and cheese, and they never have
any of that left over, which they get sick of seeing around
and wonder how it would be in the lentil soup.

My difficulty is that I can never tell where one recipe stops
and the next one starts. This means that my most delectable
dishes are not only irrevocable but impossible to duplicate.
When, as—yes, I assure you—does happen, someone says to
me, "How did you make this?" my explanation is so long and
complicated he or she stops listening.

It must be because I live alone. I always have dabs. The

only time I use things up is when I go on vacation and turn off the icebox. I am on one nonstop recipe from one summer to the next.

One summer I made the best casserole you ever tasted by putting everything in the icebox in it. The basis was a dab from a Casserole Kitchen dish, plus a bit of cream cheese, some lettuce, a can of beer—various things. It was such an extraordinary and new taste sensation that on the Shore Line train to Boston next day I tried to write down its ingredients. Then I remembered that the friend who came to dinner the night before was also going on vacation, and she'd brought the contents of her icebox. I never could remember exactly what they were, and by the time I saw her again neither could she.

Thus was a great culinary triumph lost to the world.

But I can remember my Chicken Liver Pâté. I must tell you about it. Yes, I must. It was simply delicious. Everyone said so.

Sylvia Wright's Chicken Liver Pâté

(That sounds conceited, but they all do it, and it certainly isn't anyone else's.) Take one pound of hamburger. (Yes.) Have a friend who is coming to dinner to have hamburgers and doesn't come. Have one hamburger all by yourself, feeling somewhat aggrieved, even though it is the colds season.

It's no use. I can't do this part indented. I have to tell it as it happened. Maybe I can get indented later on.

I had leftover hamburger. I went out to dinner the next day, and the day after that it seemed to me the hamburger had better be cooked before it spoiled. I was in a hurry, and

I thought I'd slosh it around in the frying pan with some onion, and if I didn't eat it all up, I could use the rest in spaghetti sauce.

Then I discovered I was out of onions.

I didn't start this in the right place.

I should have mentioned that some days before I'd had people in for cocktails and had pitted black olives as an hors d'oeuvre. I overestimated my guests' capacity for pitted black olives, because they didn't eat them all and I'd already poured the salt water which preserves them down the drain. So when I couldn't find the onions, it occurred to me to wonder what hamburger with pitted black olives cut up in it instead of onions would be like. The olives were beginning to dry out anyway.

It wasn't very good.

So I still had leftover hamburger, with pitted black olives in it. Quite a lot.

Next day I felt I was in a hamburger rut, and I bought half a pound of chicken livers. But I am thrifty by nature, so I got some onions too, thinking I'd add them to the hamburger and make it a little more palatable.

While I'm about it, I don't see why people in groceries have to be so withering when you ask for two onions. Not two pounds, two onions. I don't have a very large icebox, and I try to buy only what I need.

I had some chicken livers for dinner, but half a pound is too much for one person to eat up (oh, well, they were frozen—I couldn't buy a quarter of a pound) so there were some left over—maybe five, maybe six.

I should have mentioned that I cooked all the chicken livers, not wanting to make the same mistake I did with the hamburger. I suppose you'd like some directions on that.

Dip chicken livers in flour to which salt, pepper, and a
soupçon of curry powder have been added. (The curry
powder was just a notion. I'm scared of it and I stopped
before I'd put in enough to even have it taste. But I don't
like to leave out anything, because you never can tell.)
Fry in bacon fat. Well, I think most people know how to
cook chicken livers. And served with a green vegetable—
why not creamed chopped spinach?—chicken livers make
a delicious quick meal.

It's beginning to sound like a real recipe.

The next day (as you can gather, my social life wasn't very
sparkling at this point, which is when I concoct my most
inimitable dishes) I thought I really had to finish up that
hamburger. Another thing, mine is a very small kitchenette
in a small apartment, and when I use the food grinder I have
to attach it to a bookcase, which I have to take some of the
books out of, so when I get steamed up to the point of using
the food grinder, I try to get some good out of it and do several things at the same time.

I decided first to grind up the leftover chicken livers to
make chicken liver pâté, and then the onion for the hamburger.

You know, I think this is where the recipe really starts.

Sylvia Wright's Inimitable Chicken Liver Pâté

Grind up five or six cooked chicken livers in—let's see,
which one was it? Not the nut-butter cutter, but the next
one bigger. Come to think of it, that's the only one I ever
use. The others fall on the floor. Grind up and add to
chicken livers about a third of a fairly large onion.

Of course, later I used the rest of the onion, ground up, in
the hamburger, as well as half of the other onion.

Add salt, freshly ground black pepper, and sherry to
chicken-liver mixture. I don't know how much sherry I

39

put in. Let's say "to taste" except I don't think you should quite be able to taste it. There's a stage where you can almost taste it, but actually you taste chicken liver more.

(I'm giving up this indenting business. While I'm about it, I think I'll give up parentheses), too. To not quite taste. Please note, Irma S. Rombauer, Clementine Paddleford, Mary Frost Mabon, et al. A new cooking direction doesn't happen every day.

Adding the onion to the hamburger made me realize that I still had quite a bit of hamburger, and before I could stop myself—I felt I hadn't really gotten everything I could out of the food grinder—I put some of the leftover hamburger into the food grinder, ground it up again, and added it to the chicken liver pâté. Only about two tablespoonfuls. Now you see why I had to start with the hamburger.

That's about all there is to my chicken liver pâté—my dear, the easiest recipe imaginable—but I'd like to point out an interesting side effect. The little bits of black pitted olive that were in the hamburger looked, when they got into the pâté, just like truffles. So I had made *Chicken Liver Pâté with Mock Truffles.* I'm sure it's the first time any- one did. I never think truffles taste of much of anything, and by this time neither did the olives, so it was quite all right.

The chicken liver pâté was really pretty delicious by now, but it seemed a little dry. I didn't want to upset the delicate balance by adding any more sherry, so I thought I'd try a little mayonnaise or cream. Somehow, I didn't have either in the icebox, but I found some leftover tomato soup. I forgot to get that in earlier. It's the time sequence that confuses me when I'm trying to give a recipe. It was canned tomato soup with milk added, but not as much milk as it says on the can.

I had a dab of milk, you see, and I happen to think it tastes better that way, and of course I'm always hoping I won't have things left over. I put in about a tablespoon of the soup, and decided the pâté was perfect.

As I mentioned, everyone said it was delicious, and it must have been because there wasn't any left over.

Would you like to hear about my Beef and Spinach Tarts? No? *Please* let me tell it. I'll be quick.

I ate some of the hamburger with onions, but it seemed mere after Chicken Liver Pâté with Mock Truffles, and I couldn't finish it. There was a dab left. There was also a dab of creamed chopped spinach. So I made a little pie crust out of half a box of pie-crust mix and cut it up into more or less diamond shapes (I roll my pie crust on the coffee table). I mixed the leftover beef and spinach together and used it to fill the pie crust diamonds.

> Bake in a moderate oven until delicately brown. This recipe makes six. No,

(I forgot I wasn't going to try that (or those) again.) I think it was seven, including the undersized, rumpled one.

You know, somehow they just weren't delectable. There was too much spinach and not enough beef, and I must confess I threw most of them away. I couldn't think of anything to put *them* in. Some cooks might have poured a cheese sauce over them and served them up as a meat-saving main dish, but I don't believe in gilding the lily to that extent, particularly when it isn't a very good lily to start with. Besides, I didn't have any cheese.

But I'm not discouraged. It so happens that I have half a box of leftover pie-crust mix and half an onion and a little tomato soup. I think I'll just see what else there is in the icebox.

41

Soap and the Opera

MODERN LIFE DEMANDS BIZARRE adjustments: one of mine concerns cleaning.

Every Saturday afternoon in winter I clean my apartment to the radio broadcast of the Metropolitan Opera. I like opera. I listen to it. This is the difficulty.

If only one opera in the Metropolitan repertoire were right to clean to, once a winter I could breeze through my chores logically and precisely. I never can. Every Saturday, I leap from dusting to mopping, from scrubbing to polishing, abandoning a cloth here, a mop there, in a conscientious attempt to stick with the opera and clean at the same time.

If I were not saddled with the Metropolitan, I would clean in the following order: straighten up the room, dust Venetian blinds, clean window sills, brush lampshades and upholstered furniture, dust surfaces, mop floor where rugs aren't, vacuum rugs. Clean kitchenette. Clean bathroom, including washing floor. Odd jobs—polishing brass and silver, cleaning windows and mirrors—are sandwiched in as they fall due.

This order makes sense: it chases the dirt from above to below. But I have had to give it up, because operas don't work this way.

Consider the *Marriage of Figaro*. It opens, as an opera should, with an overture. Overtures, though many composers seem to think otherwise, are for tidying up. The overture to the *Marriage of Figaro* is one of the best: it impels you to a gay scurry, proper for the purpose. On to the Venetian blinds!

You can't. When the curtain goes up, Figaro is measuring and planning and Susanna is trying on a hat. Their music is for rearranging your furniture in different positions, or for trying on a hat, and preferably for both. And you don't have much time because soon Figaro swings into "Se vuol ballare," one of the best woodwork-washing pieces ever composed.

The opera is barely started and already my cleaning plan has been thrown off.

(Someone is wondering about bedmaking. The answer is that the opera starts at 2 P.M., and I don't want anyone to think that I am in the habit of leaving the bed unmade all morning. But it can happen, and if it does the bed should be made first. Composers do not realize this: bedmaking music always occurs when the opera is well along. The first suitable moment in the *Marriage of Figaro* is Cherubino's "Non so più cosa son, cosa faccio." This aria demands that you make the bed from scratch, that is, take everything off, turn the mattress, and change the sheets, because it begins with nervous vitality and turns tenderly reflective in time for smoothing and tucking in.

Mozart's operas are full of fine bedmaking arias. In *Don Giovanni*, one might choose "Deh vieni alla finestra" for a studio couch. Plump the pillows to the plucked accompaniment. For a king-sized double bed, the Catalogue Aria.)

How would I like an opera to open? With Venetian blinds —that is, music which requires delicacy and reaching—that is, a coloratura aria. "Caro nome" would be excellent.

Venetian-blind music is ticklish. When one is on a stepladder and a soprano flats, one grasps for the nearest thing handy. Once during the Mad Scene of *Lucia*, I brought down a whole blind. An example of Venetian-blind music par excellence is the Queen of the Night's "Die hölle Rache," but it demands great balance and control. On the other hand, Fiordiligi's "Come scoglio" in *Così fan tutte* should not be used for blinds. The gaps are too wide. If you stay with the music, you will fall. During this aria I keep my feet on the ground and dust alternately a picture and the baseboard below it. This is what it is for.

One should do Venetian blinds first, when one is fresh and alert. But how many operas open with a coloratura aria? One must fit the blinds in as the composer wills. Wagner, during the Ring Cycle, wants them dirty. The forest bird is his only Venetian-blind moment, though if one has mastered a sort of scooping motion, one can manage a few slats while Brünnhilde ho-yo-to-hoes.

When there is no overture the opera's opening chords establish one's cleaning mood. *Aïda*, which contains splendid cleaning music, opens badly with some questioning chords. They question the whole idea of cleaning. One sits down and wonders if it might not be better to put off cleaning until the next day and the Philharmonic.

The thing to do is to bide your time through "Celeste Aïda," the trio, and so forth, while making something quiet and thoughtful like an icebox cake. The real cleaning music begins with the entrance of the king, Ramfis, the priests, and Tutti. "Or, di Vulcano al tempio muovi" is a magnificent bathroom-floor-scrubbing piece, if the bathroom is not too big or the floor too dirty. With "Ritorna vincitor!" one must rest again or finish the icebox cake, for Aïda is of no use until she gets squared away with "Numi, pietà," fine for mopping up the water you left on the bathroom floor.

But if the icebox cake requires using an egg beater for

whipped cream (one of mine does), I would advise making it during the next scene. Here we are in the temple and the priestesses are singing to Immenso Fthà. I am very much against doing anything during the opera which provides a counternoise, but the opening of this scene is true egg-beater music, swively, low-keyed, and not so fast that it tires your wrist. However, the scene is also good for polishing silver, particularly some piece which has small details (song of the priestesses), and large plain areas (more vigorous song of the priests).

An even better example of egg-beater music is Senta's song in the *Flying Dutchman*, but this opera is not in the repertoire at present.

I find it interesting that two composers treating the same subject can provoke such different cleaning jobs. In *Aïda*, anyone who invokes either Isis or Osiris almost certainly provides brushing music. One cannot brush to "O Isis und Osiris" in the *Magic Flute*. For a long time I considered both this invocation and "In diesen heil'gen Hallen" too noble to clean to, but recently I came to the conclusion that one might use them for cleaning something extremely rich and grand, like a large Italian-marble coffee table.

By now you will have begun to grasp the intricacies of this problem. There is some good cleaning music in almost every opera (except *Pelléas et Mélisande*, where there is none whatsoever), but the composers scatter it planlessly here and there, and often, when they get hold of a nice cleaning bit, show a frivolous inability to stick with it until I can finish whatever it is I am doing.

What a master was Offenbach of all sorts of cleaning music! And how considerate a composer!—*Tales of Hoff-*

mann is studded with injunctions like "Je commence," "Silence," "Attention," or "Voilà," handy indications that one is about to have to switch jobs, which allow a moment to put away the broom and get out the dustpan. Yet how haphazardly is his cleaning music placed!

Act I contains, not one, but two, stirring brushing pieces, but in the middle of telling the story of Klein Zach, Hoffmann interrupts himself to dream of Stella. I must interrupt myself to cut the stems of flowers. Act II opens with a splendid scrubbing or mopping march, but the scrubbing or mopping must be started and stopped three times. In between I do the Venetian blinds with Olympia, and sort the laundry to a little waltz so intoxicating that it must be used for something abandoned. There is the Barcarolle, perfect for dusting or polishing. (If one does not dust to something lyrical and leisurely, one misses rungs.) In Act IV there is Frantz's song for complaining about cleaning.[1] There is even some nervous, ominous music for taking medicine, or one's pulse. One can get almost anything one can think of done during *Tales of Hoffmann* in the most senseless order imaginable.

Sometimes a composer makes almost impossible demands. The first act of *Rigoletto* requires superhuman spryness. Chords of grim warning, which almost say "Get on. Get on," open the opera. Cleaning is irrevocable. Gay brushing music quickly follows, and almost immediately thereafter, "Questa o quella," music for scattering. There are two possibilities: sort the laundry or clean your rugs by strewing on them one of those damp powdered rug-cleaning messes. Now you

[1] An interesting and useful selection. I can think of only two others of this type: Berta's aria in the *Barber of Seville*, with its appropriate "O che casa in confusione," and (stretching a point) Leporello's "Notte è giorno faticar."

need something to brush the rug powder in to, but instead you get a quiet and graceful little minuet with the Duke singing and you switch quickly to arranging flowers or ironing. Rigoletto begins to tease Ceprano and you begin brushing. You brush and brush and you keep it up at a furiously brisk tempo through "Tutto è gioia, tutto è festa." Suddenly Monterone enters to disturb the vile orgies. Gloom descends and with it a change of job—for instance, cleaning under the radiator. If you have been at it as Verdi would wish, you will have to. A lot of rug powder has gone under there.

The trick with *Rigoletto* is not to get up during the chorus at the end of the act. The next act opens with Sparafucile, whose music is very low down and also meant for cleaning under something. But frustration is ahead. "Caro nome" is coming up, and if your radiator, as is customary, is under your windows, you will get it all dirty again when you climb up with Gilda and wipe the dust off the Venetian blinds.

With practice (I have learned to put a newspaper over the radiator during the scene between Rigoletto and Gilda and the identification of Walter Maldé) one could adjust to the first act of *Rigoletto*. Practice is not what one gets, because next week we may have *Götterdämmerung*, an entirely different kettle of drums.

It begins with Norns and Norns are impossible to clean to. Then it continues without a break for at least an hour and a half, almost all of it possible cleaning music including top-notch bits like the oath of blood brotherhood (brush the hearth.) But it is too tiring to clean steadily through this act and the next one and the next one. In the second act, we have Hagen and Alberich, both cleaning-under-things characters, a workout with the broom (vassals), very heavy

47

scrubbing ("So soll es sein! Siegfried falle, etc."), and a good deal else.

The longer Wagner operas require another change of habit. I spend the first act of *Götterdämmerung* on some slow dirty job I have been putting off. For instance, I take all the burners off the stove and clean them with steel wool. I clean everything else in sight slowly, using Waltraute's more somber utterances for whatever is burned on. This job requires running the water in the sink occasionally, which in normal circumstances I would only do during the Opera Quiz. But with the Rhine theme Wagner has supplied snatches of built-in running-water music. If I have to run the water for any length of time, I use Siegfried's Rhine Journey.

One helpful feature of the Ring Cycle is those moments when someone sits down and tells, not only the whole story of his life, but of everyone else's. They resemble the synopses published with serials, and I think Wagner must have needed them to refresh his mind about who had borne whom by whom, where everyone was, or who had recently become a dragon. In these passages, one zips through all the leit-motifs from the previous opera, usually ending balefully with "Das Ende!" For example, in the second act of *Die Walküre*, Wotan gives a run-through of everything that happened in *Das Rheingold* for the benefit of Brünnhilde who wasn't around in the first opera.

In some cleaning jobs, like washing the outside of windows, it is difficult to hear the radio, and these synopses are just right for them. If you have washed the inside of the windows during *Das Rheingold*, next week you can pop out to do the other side as soon as Wotan sits down. But the Metropolitan also seems to be aware that repetition is involved, because they are likely to cut. In this case, just as you get settled on the sill and make a few swipes, you hear "Das Ende!" in the distance and have to come in again.

Parsifal is a real problem. It is not good cleaning music, it is tiring, because we go through everything twice, and it comes in early spring when I am in need of sulfur and molasses. *Parsifal* makes me want to sit down.

My solution may not be possible for everyone. I have an old-fashioned desk with four large drawers. Each drawer has two large brass incrustations with handles and one large keyhole incrustation, as well as other bits and pieces of brass here and there. I unscrew them all one by one, take them off, and polish them. Then I screw them back on. One should wear rubber gloves during *Parsifal*. It is hard on the hands.

What I want for the close of an opera is as specific as what I want for the beginning, and I get it just as seldom. First I want a long, dull intermission, for vacuuming and for running a bath. By now I am pretty dirty. Then an elevating finale to listen to while soaking in the bathtub. The end of Gounod's *Faust* is perfect: the harmonies are so uplifting one hardly needs soap. I also like the sextet at the end of *Don Giovanni*. Its opening is fresh, exact, and sudsy. Fugues are very nice for washing. Even though one is worn out with the terror of the Don's finish and the effort of cleaning, one feels that life can begin anew. But unfortunately it is not preceded by an intermission, and it is much too short. How could Mozart have known that I don't like to take a bath in five minutes?

In the fullness of time and the march of the operas, everything will eventually get done. But one must accept the fact that there are certain pieces of music one cannot clean to,

49

and that one may have to wait some time before being able to go at a specific task.

Besides Norns, one cannot clean to the following: Erda, Gurnemantz, Boris Godounov either giving political instruction about alliances with Lithuania or going mad, and *Electra*. If you try to clean to *Electra*, you will have a nervous breakdown. Vassals, Valkyries, apprentices, choir boys (*Tosca*), sailors, Figaros, and any happy peasants provide good cleaning music.

In Italian opera anything which begins zitti, zitti, or basta, basta, or piano, piano, or even piano pianissimo, as in the opening of the *Barber of Seville*, is intended for brushing.

The perfect selection for carpet sweeping is the chorus in the first act of *I Pagliacci*, which opens "Din, don." Although this chorus seems to be an effort to get everyone into church, I know it is for carpet sweeping because it is introduced by several vigorous "Andiam's," intended to get me started.

The Siege of Kazan in *Boris Godounov* is for sweeping with a broom. The Anvil Chorus in *Il Trovatore* stumps me. Clearly it is meant for beating rugs in the back yard, but this is a dated form of cleaning, not possible in a small apartment.

There is one moment in the opera repertoire when you can run a sewing machine. If you can do it while giggling and thinking about love, so much the better. This, of course, is the atelier scene in *Louise*.

Puccini arias are perfect for ironing. One needs a lush, lyrical, isolated selection to get one through a cotton blouse or dress. Puccini is particularly good if one does not have a steam iron and has to dampen things. One can cry automatically, gently, and without despair, which helps in the dampening.

But the Flower Duet in *Madame Butterfly* should be

saved for extra-special efforts to fix up your place, flowers, candles, and even, if you have one, running up a flag.

Salome's Dance should be used for going through the closet and throwing out clothes. If you have the courage, it will serve you well, because you *have* to throw something out. The frenzied drive of the dance prevents any second thoughts like "This might come back into fashion," or "I *could* change that neckline."

Anyone who has not heard from me for a long time should not give up hope. The Metropolitan is reviving *Eugen Onegin*, and I will be my usual adaptable self during the letter scene.

My compromise with the Metropolitan is complete, but I continue to dream about the perfect opera. In fact, I am working on the libretto, and any composer who is interested should get in touch with me. There is one proviso, and he won't like it: I must be allowed to say how long each aria, chorus, etc., will take. But it will be inexpensive to produce, since it will require only one set—my apartment.

It opens with a spirited overture, during which the curtain is down. Behind it, I am rushing around getting the place neat enough to be on public view. When the curtain rises, I am discovered on top of a stepladder cleaning the Venetian blinds and singing my coloratura aria. The aria will be novel. It will begin on a high note and work its way down. It will be an *aria da capo*, because I have three windows, one of them (the middle section) longer than the others. During the tumultuous applause, I will brush off the window sills.

The baritone enters. He has evil designs on me, the first of which is to make me stop cleaning and pay attention to him. I spurn him. He argues. I explain. He argues some more. This is a brisk recitative, and I brush off the top of the radiator. After this, the baritone launches into an aria of denunciation and rage, which calls on his lowest chest tones. I clean under the radiator. When I get up, we sing a contrapuntal duet, during which I try to put the dustpan and brush back in my closet and he tries to stop me. Thwarted, he exits, and we hear him singing "Maledetto" outside the door. (Excuse me, it will be the English equivalent, which I regret to say is "Curses.")

Tension and suspense are more thoroughly built into the plot of this opera than that of any other. If Baritone manages to prevent my getting the apartment cleaned, the opera cannot end.

I am upset by the baritone, and I am aware that I must have a mezzo-soprano. During a delicate intermezzo, in which descending sixteenth notes on the violins indicate my uncertainty, I go to the telephone and call my best friend, who lives upstairs. She says she will be right down; she is right down, and she is a mezzo.

I greet her and we begin a charming feminine duet, during which we discuss the behavior of the baritone (with whom she is secretly in love, but I suspect it), and whether Glass Wax, Windex, or soap and water are better for cleaning mirrors and the glass over pictures. She demonstrates how she does it (I can use a little help). I show her my method. We comment on both methods. The aria is climaxed by a happy burst of agreement in a major key—her method is better.

After a brief orchestrial interlude, we finish the mirrors and seize the opportunity of their being sparkling clean to look at ourselves in them. Then, in a slow, plaintive duet in the related minor, we wonder about our looks and whether the tenor and the baritone love, respectively, us.

This is the Mirror Duet, and as far as I know it is unique

in opera, because we both have our backs to the prompter. I will arrange the mirrors so that we can see him.

A comic interlude ensues with the entrance of the Fuller Brush man, a basso, to allow me to clean the baseboards. In the delightful Brush Song, characterized by the refrain, "Accept this sample," with its amusing bassoon accompaniment, he displays his wares, and attempts to get Mezzo to buy a Venetian-blind brush. The three of us then sing a gay trio, in which Mezzo tries to explain that I use a dustcloth for the blinds; the Fuller Brush man continues to argue; and I finish the baseboards.

The Fuller Brush man departs, and I go into the kitchenette to wash the cloths I have used to clean the blinds, the mirrors, and the baseboards. While I am thus occupied, my friend sings an aria about the baritone with a fugal orchestral accompaniment to which I scrub. This is another effect which I believe is unique in opera. It may, in fact, be impossible.

Enter the tenor. Mezzo, who is tactful, exits to a scurrying motif in the violins. Tenor has brought me a bunch of freesias. While I cut the stems and arrange them in a vase (I want a spurt of running water music here), we join in a romantic duet in praise of flowers, spring, our dreams for the future, and our earnest hope that I will get the apartment cleaned by the end of the afternoon so that the opera can end and we can go out and have a delicious dinner. Ominous chords in the brasses suggest that Baritone will do everything in his power to prevent this.

I am sorry if your interest has been aroused, but I am not going to tell you any more. Someone might steal my plot. It is intricate; something is going on every minute, and I clean

53

everything. I even clean during the choruses, when a group of my friends comes in, because they have heard me on the radio and want to see how I am coming along. Wait a minute, who's on the radio? Am I cleaning to myself?

We had better not explore this.

The opera ends with the famous (it will be) Bath Sextet. The principals, except me, are gathered in my living room. I am in the bathtub. I am visible to the audience, but not to the other singers, a tantalizing scene, which might sell out the opera. Someone is singing to me through the half-open bathroom door, and you will be surprised to learn who it is. Baritone. I have had a revulsion of feeling against Tenor, who is more interested in my getting my cleaning done than in me. Baritone is singing to me about me. I am singing to him about him, and about how nice it is to take a bath. Tenor and Mezzo have discovered interests in common, and they are singing about how nice the apartment looks and what the best cleaning methods are. They are happy. Baritone and I are going on to higher things. The Fuller Brush man is trying to sell me a bath brush.

Who, you would like to know, is the sixth person in the sextet? That is the cleaning woman whom I am going to hire to come in next week.

Dear Fiduciary Trust Company

YOU SOUND CROSS. HOW, YOU COLDLY ask, can anyone have spent so much more money than she told the Fiduciary Trust Company she was going to? Don't think, you intimate to me, that you can play fast and loose with funds, even if they are your own funds.

Your tone of letter indicates that for you this is standard procedure. You assume you are something quite usual, even something I should accept. I can't. I find you peculiar.

Look at it from my point of view. Here is our family, owning a delightful, if dilapidated, house by the seashore. I own a sixth, and my brother owns a twelfth, and one of my aunts owns a third, and the other of my aunts owns five-twelfths. Things are simple.

My aunt who owns the third dies, and things are still simple because I am expecting to inherit it. Suddenly you leap into the picture, and it's your third of a house. I have inherited it, but you have it, in trust, for me.

You don't know anything about the house. You've never seen it. You don't intend to see it. You don't know its beautiful view of the Sound ("We must cut down that dead tree"). You've never been swimming here ("It's the getting in that's difficult"), or felt the breeze on the piazza in summer ("This must be a scorcher on the mainland"). You don't know the house's individual smell—wood, salt air, soap, and something else. You haven't struggled with the bad habits of the privet roots: they crawl into the drainpipes and awful things transpire (I use this exactly) in the cellar. And you have no notion of my Aunt Maria, who knows where everything is and the minute it isn't. It is Aunt Maria who established how things are put away for the winter: ink bottles are put in the potties that have covers, in case they freeze and burst. If they do, you can always wash the potties, and if they don't, there is your ink for next summer.

Incidentally, you will be glad to hear that the bottle of Noxon which burst last winter did no damage to your third of the laundry.

Through no virtue of yours or effort on your part, you acquired a third of a summer house in a desirable location. Were you pleased? Did you politely thank anyone? You carped. You told me trust companies don't like property that doesn't produce income.

We amiably decided that we would rent for the summer and produce income. We did rent and we did produce income, but we had to make a few alterations—rewiring, etc.—which we had been putting off. We happened to spend more than we produced.

Do you commiserate? Do you say, "Better luck next time?" No, you want to know why you weren't told of this ahead of time. I didn't know ahead of time myself, but this doesn't satisfy you. I have to explain.

Meanwhile you sit in New York, and take a two-per-cent commission from me for making me explain how I spent some money that is really mine, but that you keep and take two per cent of for letting me spend and explaining how and why I spent it.

Do you wonder I sometimes ask myself if a third of me is in trust?

(Is it?)

Even a third of me couldn't make a long-distance telephone call every time I had to throw out a broken bottle of Noxon. Sometimes it was physically impossible for me to do so, like being in the act of tying up mattresses which had to be done over while being told about the rot under the piazza.

On an island, things are complicated: they have to go to the mainland to be fixed. I couldn't manage the two mattresses on my bicycle, so I had to order a truck to take them to the boat.

Even though I am not a trust company, I am thrifty, and I had decided the ticking would do for a while longer. The minute I had called the truck, I realized that when the mattresses were delivered to the boat, they would be thrown down on the dirty wet deck. To avoid the ticking being ruined, I had to wrap them up.

Have you ever tried to package two mattresses in a hurry so their ticking won't get dirty in the hold of a boat? If not, this is what happens. Just when you get a mattress curled around and roped with the old clothesline, the clothesline breaks. The mattress gives you a smart blow and knocks you on the floor (we had been on the bed). Downstairs, Jack Peterson, the carpenter, is calling to you that the rot under the piazza is much worse than we realized, and will you please come and look at it. Being what he is, he sounds both doomed and gratified. At this point, if you were not a company, you would cry.

That explains why you were charged for a third of a new clothesline. I used old sheets to cover the mattresses, so you're not out anything on packaging. Aunt Maria saved you money, too. She keeps old hair pillows and mattresses, because it is good hair and may come in handy. So, although there was an extra charge of forty-four cents for carting the pillows to the boat, you were saved about six dollars per mattress for new hair.

The pillows were before your time, and I don't believe a third of them really belonged to you. I could make a case for your owing the rest of us something on the saving on hair. I intend to be magnanimous, but I point this out in case you think your accounts are any more complicated than mine. I may have to take into consideration that Aunt Maria will think the pillows were before my time, too, in which case I will have to deduct my sixth of the saving from my share of the total cost. I think that's what I'll have to do.

What's more, you saved on bicycle wrapping. Don't worry about what happened to the mattresses on the way back. The mattress company packed them in brown paper envelopes. I kept the envelopes in case they should come in handy, and when the tenants were about to arrive and I had to put my bicycle away in the cellar, one of the envelopes was just right for putting a bicycle away in a cellar in.

I am saving the other mattress envelope, of which you own a third, and if you have any use for it, I will be glad to send it to you. If, that is, you will pay the postage.

Now that you have forced me to go over the way we do things, I realize that you may find us strange. It is unsettling enough to have to justify one's habits to another person, who has a few of his own. How can one explain them to a company, which has nothing but? Some of mine are acquired, some inherited, and some were thrust upon me, like the mattress. You would understand this better is you could stop being a company for a moment, but I know that would be illegal.

I will try to explain.

Like many places and families, this one prides itself on being unique, and is only a little peculiar. The people who come for the summer are rich, and the people who live here all year round are comfortable from looking after the rich ones. The two groups are not as different as they think, except that from June 15 to Labor Day, the local people have no time to talk, and the summer people have plenty.

But now is the season when the air is so clear that the houses on the mainland are miraged, when the ocean is a deep blue, and the long grass is turning lavender; now is the season when the silence of no summer people settles over the island. It is a time for leisurely conversations about fishing, rich people, bittersweet, and other things we have here, a time for sitting by the fire in the evenings, a time for explaining to the Fiduciary Trust Company. (Please bear with me. I'm giving you atmosphere, so you will realize that I'm as real as you are.)

It is also the season for looking over other people's houses and gardens. If, like us, they put things away carefully, it is only mildly interesting: when you peer in windows you see old sheets draped on things. The gardens, however, are gratifying. I never take anything if I think someone is coming back for a weekend, unless I know the tomatoes wouldn't last till then. But, observing such courtesies, one enjoys good salads in the fall.

Knowing that you may misinterpret this, I would not have brought it up, except to make clear to you that I have surveyed a lot of houses. I have looked at other people's rot, and in some newer houses it is much worse than ours. This explains why you have no reason to complain about spending a hundred and ninety dollars on fixing one section of the porch, after seventy years. There are twelve other sections, and you must get used to it.

We don't call it a house. Even though it has eight bedrooms, we call it a cottage. Cottages are ample and rambling and were built about 1880. They have acres of roof on different levels, from which shingles are detached in hurricanes, creating work for carpenters. You haven't run into this yet. It is even more expensive than everything else here, which is very. A can of salted peanuts costs forty-six cents.

One reason why things are expensive is that, like nuns and sailors elsewhere, workmen come in pairs. There are always two carpenters, two painters, and two plumbers. In the case of Jack Peterson, this coupling is sound. You would like him because he knows ahead of time that there is more rot than is visible. Termites are inevitable to him. If he didn't come with another carpenter for mitigation, I would cut my throat.

It might be easier for me if you got someone to pair off with.

(No matter what he says, there are no termites in the cellar. Try as he would, all he could find was a few rotted boards he said were a termite trap if I didn't remove them.)

The painters come from the mainland, and arrive off a fishing boat at twenty minutes of eight while I am wandering around the house in a wrapper in a fog. Since they are here, there is little point in my telling them it isn't a good idea to paint in a fog. I wouldn't in any case, because they are gloomy already. It is a long time before they will be home, and they need each other for comfort.

The plumbers wouldn't have to come in pairs except for the crawl space, which is under the kitchen and has always presented a problem. The head plumber is big, burly, and equable, and I am in love with him, because in the kind of life I have been leading, a serene plumber is a father figure. You might have been a father figure, too, if you had wanted to, but you're too picky. The head plumber is much bigger than I am, and I had trouble in the crawl space myself when I was considerably smaller. Once he is in there, he has to have someone to hand him things. This is as good an explanation as I can give as to why it cost sixty dollars to fix the pipes under the kitchen sink.

It didn't occur to me to question things coming in pairs, because so many things in the house do. There are two Delft tiles, held up by hooks, on either side of the living-room mantelpiece, which also has two vases and two candlesticks. Every winter the tiles, which were bought by my grandparents on a European trip, are put away in a certain box, wrapped in a certain newspaper. It is in Dutch, is dated 1895, and the only headline I can read announces the death of Friedrich Engels. Aunt Maria again, of course. Aunt Maria has a coin purse with slots, and she always puts the coins in heads up and facing in the same direction. She gets uneasy if she has, say, Jefferson and Indian-head nickels, because the heads look opposite ways. I know about being punctilious, and there is no need for you to behave as if I had never heard of it.

Most of the pictures in the house come in pairs. There are two Romes (Colosseum and Castel Sant' Angelo), two sepia English cathedrals, two colored steeplechases, two hunting dogs, and two Dumas characters fighting duels, one indoors, one outdoors. There is Courtship and Marriage.

Evangeline, however, is unique. Evangeline is an engraving, "Dedicated by Permifsion to Profefsor Longfellow."

"Sat by some nameless grave and thought that perhaps in its bosom, / He was already at rest and she longed to slumber beside him," it says underneath. There are weeping willows and she sits on the gravestone staring at the ground. This picture has always been in my room, and has made me mournful for years, particularly when it is raining.

I mention Evangeline to illustrate the quality of my difficulties in getting the house ready for the tenants. If I had done more painting and carpentering myself, I might have saved money. But I simply didn't have time. Throwing things out and putting things away took too long.

Neither sounds difficult and I'm sure neither would have occurred to you. They don't show in any way a trust company can see, like money.

Aunt Maria made a special visit to help throw things away. She knew we had to.

But she had a sentiment about Evangeline.

I've already told you about old hair pillows.

One does not get rid of a chair with a broken cane seat, even if it has not been fixed in fifteen years, when it matches a whole chair. They go together.

Old laced canvas bathing shoes may come in handy for guests who haven't brought their own, not realizing our rocks are barnacley.

There was the old-fashioned large round tin bathtub which was always kept under the double bed in the downstairs spare room. Usually a single male guest has this room, because Aunt Maria thinks it is nice and separate for him. He is supposed to find the old tin tub convenient to put his bathing suit in after swimming. That he never does is no reason to get rid of it.

There was the thing, and even Aunt Maria didn't know

exactly what it was for. It was small, square, and made of wood, with one flat side and an open box built onto the bottom of the flat side. Or top, as the case may be, since it's doubtful which side should be up. Aunt Maria couldn't remember what it was for, but, now that she had seen it, she said, she realized it had always been there. It was a nice little thing. She had a sentiment about it. Perhaps you could stand a plant on it.

Those small embroidered squares, all different, go under finger bowls. One *might* use finger bowls sometime.

The candleholders with springs in them are for the dining-room table. They hold paper shades with dangling bead fringe, and a silver filigree shade goes on top of that. It seemed too bad when they had been kept for so long—

For your information, all these things are now in the large closet on the third floor.

I find Aunt Maria catching: when I dug out my grandfather's large glass tobacco jar, I decided it would do for cookies. You will not be much interested to hear that it does nicely for the kind you want to keep moist, but not for the kind you want to keep crisp. Unfortunately, this happens to be a device one doesn't need at the seashore.

Just because I took a little time out to make cookies, don't jump to the conclusion I wasn't concentrating. I concentrated the whole time on saving money, but it did no good. Our house has intransigences.

Take the kitchen. I admit I should have told you ahead of time about cutting through into the china closet. I didn't decide until a carpenter was there (shelves) and then it was too late to consult you. Now you own a third of a doorway instead of a third of a slide, the little opening that was there before.

63

This is why we went so far over on the estimate for linoleum. Once a doorway was created, the linoleum couldn't just stop at the doorway: it had to go on. And if there was linoleum in the china closet, there had to be linoleum in the kitchen pantry, too, to balance.

Now the reason why the linoleum was not linoleum, but vinyl tile, which is more expensive, was because I was concentrating on saving money. So was my cousin, who was helping me decide on colors. The fact that neither of us could stand the colors the other picked didn't increase the expense. We couldn't stand the expensive ones, too.

I had never thought about linoleum, and when I did I realized that no one ever had before. Linoleum is one of the few things in this world that never looks like itself. It looks like sculptured rugs, Aubusson carpets, bricks, finger painting, or Jackson Pollocks.

I had just decided on a Jackson Pollock, which was called spatter pattern, when they told me that linoleum lasts ten or fifteen years, and must be waxed regularly.

I was amazed. What was the point of it?

I pointed out that I never waxed the floor in the kitchen, which, being wood stained dark, didn't show the dirt. I pointed out that it had lasted seventy years. Jack Peterson said wood floors were insanitary, because of dirt in the cracks. I said we didn't eat off the floor, and no one had died. He likes to argue for its own sake, so here he got off the track. He told me the only really good heavy-duty floor was wood, which they use in the kitchen of the Club where twenty or thirty people work.

That proved my point, but not to him, because he hastily told me that at the Club they washed the floor twice a day with soap and boiling water. Was I prepared to do that? he asked accusingly.

He and everyone agreed that linoleum shows the dirt and has to be washed and waxed and wears out quickly, and was going to be a job to lay because our floors are wavy, but, they said, if you rent, you must have linoleum. Linoleum is pretty.

By this time, I didn't like any of the linoleum patterns, and my cousin wanted something pink, which I couldn't spend even half my life with. We had to compromise, and we did, on black and white tiles, which looks like tile, but aren't. The white tiles look as if something gray had been spilled on them, which means they don't show the dirt, except that something comes off if I rub them with steel wool. But, they tell me, if I don't fuss at it and wax it once in a while, it may last my lifetime.

So next to wood, which has lasted my lifetime, it seemed the best thing. Can't you see now that I tried?

I'm not sure if this explains everything, but it shows why it has taken me so long to. One of my problems has been how much to tell you: I would have a better grasp of this if I weren't confused about what or who you are.

I was clear that you are a company, an odd company because you are set up to mind, not your own business, but mine. This means seizing any money you can get and investing it for my benefit at three or four per cent—strange to start with because if I could seize any money I could get six per cent for it. But you can't help that. You are what the law says you must be, and the law is precedent. You, therefore, are precedented. I, of course, am unprecedented. Some sort of polar relationship should be possible.

As you may have gathered, I decided that my way in this relationship should be to be as unprecedented as possible. As yet I'm not very good at it. But I felt it might be developing for me, and good experience for you.

65

But just when I get things going, you throw me off. You behave like a person. You accuse, or something like that.

Are you clear about yourself, Fiduciary Trust Company? I have at hand (it has taken a little time to write all this) your annual report. You begin by quoting an "eminent physician" who once said, "We must . . . treat the disease according to the best medical knowledge. But we must also never, never forget that we are taking care of a human being." I gather he needed to reassure himself at certain moments, such as when he was treating a human being with parrot fever. You go on to say that "the relationship between doctor and patient applies equally to our relationship with our clients." Then you talk earnestly about your spirit of helpfulness, sympathy, understanding, and so on.

What makes you think you're a doctor? It's insulting—I'm not sick in relation to you. Why are you pretending to be a person? Is it a backhanded attempt to get my sympathy?

If it is, I consider it beneath you and U.S. Steel and various other companies that have tried this with me. As a company, you should be asympathetic. This would relieve the pressure on me as well as on you.

Perhaps you should sit down and have a files-to-files talk with yourself. You're limited, you know, by definition. You can't be everything. Remember that you are a company, and don't go creeping around corners like a human being.

I refuse to feel sorry for you. After all, as Aunt Maria says, you chose to do it. You could have been the Cockaigne Light and Power Company, Erewhon Underwear, or Utopian Utensils. You had a choice and you chose to be the Fiduciary Trust Company. Though limited, it sounds like a solid thing to be. Have the courage of your corporation.

My Kitchen Hates Me

EVER SINCE I HAD TO LIE FLAT ON MY stomach on the kitchen floor to see if the broiler was lighted in our new stove, I've wondered about the modern kitchen. I don't say it isn't a dream kitchen with space-saving features to give the busy housewife (me) extra leisure. I don't say it isn't a hundred per cent more efficient that the old kitchen. But I'm used to inefficiency. I don't recognize efficiency until it rises up and smites me.

That is just what it keeps doing.

The oven of the new stove is somewhere around your knees. You light the broiler by sticking a match through a little hole in the bottom of the oven. It's drafty down there, and the first time the draft blew out the match. This is why I was flat on the floor peering into the broiler. When I saw it wasn't lighted, I tried again. Gas had collected, of course. It smote me.

The old stove was black, and looked distinctly dated, like nineteen-twenties dresses. In fact, it looked like a nineteen-twenties girl, perched on long, thin, bowlegged legs. The oven was at the left of the burners, and the bottom of it was on the *same level*. You could look a popover in the eye without snapping a garter or slipping a disk.

Before that stove I dimly remember another, also black. The whole of it was warm the whole time—it contained a real wood fire, which made the kitchen quite cozy. You could put food in a pan, stick it on the stove, and warm it up just a little and it never stuck to the bottom of the pan. You always had boiling water ready because there was a teakettle at the back. You could dump the garbage in and let it burn up.

Things are more convenient now. You just push the garbage down the drain (except large bones) and then you put on the cover, turn on the water, and wait. Don't relax, though. Once a cherry stone got caught in the part that grinds, and it sounded like Bastogne. I've had a nervous tic ever since.

These are nervous times and one must accept them. Like the infrared broiler. The first time I turned it on, I fancied it was a sort of death ray, such as Killer Kaine in *Buck Rogers in the Twenty-fifth Century* used. I wondered what the symptoms of death-ray poisoning were. I've gotten used to it.

I do have a scaly place on the back of my hand—

Having a nice white easy-to-keep-clean porcelain sink is something every modern woman should thank her stars she is not her grandmother about (my grandmother paid three dollars a week for someone to wash the dishes and do a few other things, like ironing a clean starched petticoat every day, but anyway). I don't regret the old soapstone sink one bit. It was handy to be able to sharpen the paring knife on the edge of it. You could use it as a scrubbing board when you washed the dish towels. Of course you had to keep it scrubbed up with Sapolio. But it never *looked* clean the way the porcelain ones do after you've scrubbed them as hard as you can with something with foaming action.

And dishwashers. They are another of the fabulous things

My Kitchen Hates Me

in modern kitchens. I love the dishwasher. I was so fascinated the first time we used it that after it got well started I leaned over it to listen to it churning. It didn't occur to me it would open up and bop me in the nose. Or pant warm damp air all over me.

Sometimes I feel these gadgets hate me. The dishwasher leaves little spots all over the silver just to spite me. No, no, I don't want to go back to the old soapstone sink. Though you could hear yourself think in the kitchen in those days.

I truly do love the washing machine. There is something both conscientious and abandoned about the way it swivels its internal hips while churning up all that black water. The black water is the trouble. Once you have a washing machine, you wash things it never before occurred to you to wash, and it always makes the water as black as possible to demonstrate what a pig you were pre-washing-machine. You become its minion, and it begins to lay down the law about what it will and will not do. I tried to feed a small rug into the wringer of mine, and it chattered at me angrily.

Of course I don't want to go back to the dirty, germy old days when it would never have occurred to me to wash a rug.

I was *glad* to see the last of the kitchen table. Who wants a kitchen table when they can have a working surface? A working surface is much better to work at—standing up. It's hard to sit at. You can't get your legs under it. But why should I make myself old before my time?

Anyway there isn't anything to sit on.

I'm being unfair—there is something. It's a sort of chair, but it's not very comfortable because your feet dangle and the back is so short that it barely supports your coccyx. And it's a little too high for the working surface. When I looked more closely, I saw it was really a stepladder waiting to be opened up. If you're not quite sure just where a thing is going to open up. . . . Finally, I gave it a hard yank. . . . I was supposed to get a new prescription for glasses anyway. And I don't suppose anyone but some fussy one like me minds sitting down in a nice clean dress where your feet have just been.

It's so clean in a modern kitchen that the people who designed the chair ladder must have difficulty imagining anything getting dirty, even the bottom of your shoes. At one time, modern kitchens became too clean. They used to be mostly white porcelain, but now they're pink or green, or even wood color so they will have the warmth of the old-fashioned kitchen. We used to have an old-fashioned kitchen which was entirely wood color. As a matter of fact, it was entirely wood.

I'm not so old-fashioned that I believe in dirty old wood all over a kitchen, but it had one advantage: you could put up a hook. There's no place for this in a modern kitchen. I know because I went around with a hammer and nail, tapping the kitchen's chest, and all I did was to chip off paint and then reach bedrock—some sort of metal.

One isn't supposed to need hooks in a modern kitchen. But what about pot holders? In our old kitchen we kept them on a hook next to the stove. There isn't any such hook in the modern kitchen. There aren't any pot holders either. My theory about this used to be that just before the magazine photographer took the picture, his assistant ran frantically around, removing all the pot holders. (This is the same assistant who rushes around putting baskets—bowls are out of date—of fruit on things, and sometimes in his mad career tossing a bunch of parsley or radishes onto a working surface so you'll have a notion of what goes on in this room.)

Suddenly it came to me. The modern housewife doesn't use the old-fashioned pot holder. She wears one of those aprons with a quilted mitten, which is a pot holder, attached by a long tape to the belt. There's a pocket to keep it in when not in use. This is quite an invention if you have a hook-less kitchen. Now I think of it, it opens up all sorts of possibilities for hanging things on the housewife when there is no place for them elsewhere.[1]

Dish towels were another problem. They, I discovered, hang inside something you have to open, where they're out of the way. They used to be out of the way and handy hanging on a wooden rack above the sink.

Modern kitchens are wonderful about places to put things, though I never seem to find any place to keep paper bags. Modern kitchens are solid cupboard—I beg your pardon, storage unit. This gives them a somewhat bleak shut look, which is why you need the fruit. The other thing you can have is an eggplant.

But that's the only food you see. Everything else is shut away in a storage unit. Our grandparents, who didn't know about step saving, were crude by comparison. They left things *in full view*. In my grandmother's house there was a screened cupboard, which you could see right into. In my

[1] I have given these two paragraphs serious thought, and I see nothing for it but a footnote. Since I first wrote this description, someone has invented magnetic pot holders. (Throwing them at the stove is one of the best games in a long time.) If I thought I could keep up with the manufacturers, I would rewrite the two paragraphs, but I don't. By the time this book comes out, they will have invented a plug-in housewife on casters, and the whole article will be obsolete.

grandmother's house, if you wanted a can of tomato soup you had to walk clear into the pantry and take it off a shelf.

Things are simpler now. You open the chair ladder and climb on it and open the storage unit and get out the can and get down from the ladder. And there you are. All you need to do is shut the ladder up again and put it away.

Any fool ought to be able to remember to shut a storage unit. Or any fool will get concussion of the brain.

You've seen those pictures with white lines zooming around showing how many steps the homemaker saves in a modern kitchen. I'm wondering how they figure out the up and down. I bet they don't.

But there's no denying that modern kitchens are space-saving. Some of them have a thing called a peninsula, which swoops into the middle of the kitchen. It has both counter space on top and storage units underneath.

This reminds me of the slide in my grandmother's house. The slide was a little door about a yard wide, at counter-space level. When it was open, there was a continuous shelf extending from the pantry (off the kitchen) into the china closet (off the dining room). The cook put the dishes through the slide, and the waitress got them on the other side. When there wasn't any cook or waitress any more, things became rather a scramble. I would put a dish through the slide from the kitchen side, and then race back through the kitchen, through the back hall, into the front hall, into the dining room, into the china closet, get the—it had been— hot dish, and take it back into the dining room.

Modern conveniences obviate such unnecessary steps. The peninsula is an improvement. If you haven't someone on the other side to push things to, you just walk around it. You walk back. . . .

In my grandmother's house we gave up and ate in the kitchen. This is just what you do in modern kitchens, usually at a snack bar. Some snack bars are a new kind of working surface which you can get your legs under. But you must become adjusted to the notion of never looking the rest of the family in the face. There are fewer germs this way. At a snack bar, the family lines up like birds on a telegraph wire, facing a wall (with ample electric outlets) and with their backs to the homemaker, whose life all these new devices enrich. I haven't figured out what she does if the snack bar is the only working surface. Makes sandwiches in the sink, I guess.

I feel sure that in the kitchen of the future they'll iron out the bugs I've mentioned. There will be a special bug-ironing machine. They haven't yet perfected a modern kitchen which is efficient enough so that you can leave it alone and eat in the dining room, though they get around this by calling a corner of the kitchen a dining area. But there's hope. I notice that some of the most modern kitchens have a little door at counter-space level between the kitchen and the dining room. You just push the dishes through. They've also invented a whole table you can push into the dining room after you have set it in the kitchen. Pretty soon maybe you'll be able to push the stove through and just cook your meals in the dining room.

Think of the steps *that* would save.

I Won't Do It Myself

I CAN MAKE MY OWN PLASTIC PLANTS, copper pictures, paintings without a brush, and a winter coat out of a blanket, if I happen to have an old blanket that looks like a winter coat.

I can hang my own wallpaper, personalize my own glassware, lay mosaic tiles, make my own Murray Space Shoes, construct a wheelbarrow planter box or a provincial swivel-top TV stand.

I can make things I never knew I needed, like a garbage-can coaster, by following the instructions in Bulletin No. 3 provided by the Shellac Information Bureau as a public service. I can finish by waxing and buffing the garbage-can coaster—I, who have never even waxed and buffed a garbage can.

If I send for a book called *Basket Pioneering*, and some reed, I can make Tasket Basket, the Tray of Many Uses, one of which must be to hold taskets, once you have discovered what they are.

I can learn to play the Wurlitzer organ by myself in one evening, and it doesn't surprise me that I am by myself.

I can even decorate myself myself: with the Deluxe Shell-craft Kit, I can make more than seventeen different pieces of exotic shellcraft jewelry.

I learned about these things, and many others, at a Do-It-Yourself Show. I left the show feeling that I could do anything myself. I merely needed to buy something, often called a kit, take it home, and knock it up, which means putting everything in it together.

This handy method saves the manufacturers the trouble and expense of crating or packing whatever it is, as is. In return for the saving, they offer me free the opportunity to feel creative, as long as I follow their directions letter by letter.

I started with a lamp. When finished, it was to be one of those illuminated paper beehives standing on very small legs. It arrived in a neat, cardboard envelope, knocked down flat like an opera hat, with instructions attached. (An opera hat is an artifact which might be considered a forerunner of the do-it-yourself movement.)

The first instruction was to open up the shade until it was fully expanded and turn the larger opening toward me. Unlike an opera hat, the shade had no device which kept it popped out, so I was holding it apart with both hands, when I peered over my shoulder at Instruction 2, and it said, "Take a leg."

There was a period of a certain breathlessness. Legs stuck out between my fingers in all directions like knitting needles. There were more directions. I shuffled the legs. I crossed my fingers. Something happened and a moment arrived when I was holding several things in place at once and the directions said, "Lock with knurled nut."

I was lost. What was knurled nut, and where? I wondered if it were the thing I had thought was "nibble on socket," now well buried in legs. The dictionary was on the other side of the room and, if I had been able to get to it, I would have had to turn the pages with my teeth. I couldn't move my hands.

Then I discovered knurled nut. It was locking my fingers together.

There is only one way to be creative when you knock things up. This is to create yourself six fingers on each hand and three sets of teeth, one to turn pages, one to pick up knurled nut with, and the third to grit. All these are necessary in the final acrobatic apotheosis, which always depends on locking everything in sight together with one nut. If you can locate it, it has just fallen off the table onto the floor.

I decided it might be less intense to make things from scratch, so I got some patterns for making furniture. The patterns consist of a number of oddly shaped pieces of newsprint, identified by different numbers of round holes pierced in them. In the directions, the manufacturer doesn't refer to the patterns as 0, 00, 000. Instead, he supplies you with an identification chart in which you discover that 0 is A, 00 is B, and so on. This extra step is to distract your attention so you won't be annoyed at having spent fifty cents or a dollar for some pieces of newsprint. And remember that you can always try them in your player piano.

But a lot of thought has gone into the directions. They go like this:

Trace top, bottom, and sides of pattern A on ¾-inch-thick plywood. Cut 4 pieces 11 5/4 × 25/19 inch. Channel out for sliding doors, using hand router plane or dado set in table saw. Note: the width of the grooves is 15/62 inch. The depth of the grooves is 62/15 inch. Chamfer top, bottom, and front edges. See Diagram 1. Draw parallel line 1 21/4 inch from top edge to outside edge of B. Bore hole 1 inch from inside edge. Assemble A and B using glue, or if plaster, 1/159 inch buck and wing toggle bolt. Miter. Chamfer. Sand. Your tasket is now finished.

Diagram 1 looks like this:

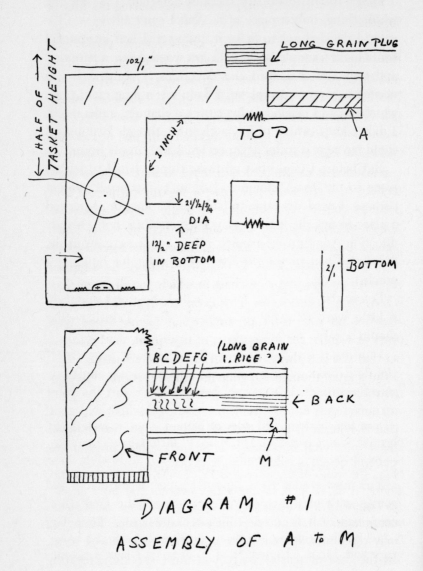

DIAGRAM #1

ASSEMBLY OF A to M

Don't try to make this, because Diagram 1 is not the whole thing, only a piece of it. And I can't advise you because I decided not to make it quite yet. I had imagined I could make a simple tasket with just wood, a saw, a hammer, and nails. After I read the directions, I realized I also needed a hand router plane, a dado set, a long grain plug, which means I needed a plug cutter, a chamfer, and a miter. I didn't know where to buy a chamfer, though I suppose I could have got a miter at an ecclesiastical supply house.

But before I could buy all these things, I had to have a place to put them. Some sort of make-it-yourself cabinet perhaps. I needed a table to make the cabinet on. I needed a place to put the table, so I needed another room. Handy directions for turning a porch into a room were available, but first I had to get the handy directions for building a porch.

Before starting to build the porch, I thought I might do a little work on what was already there. Painting—that should be easy.

Painting is easy, as long as you don't do it properly. If you do it properly, it's very difficult because you must prepare the surface. Professional painters don't, but the paint manufacturers are so afraid that do-it-yourselfers will goof, that they make it perfectly clear that *they* are not responsible (". . . vital importance of proper surface preparation. SUCCESS is assured only if all instructions . . .")

You must sand with 000 Garnet paper, repair cracks and gouges with plastic wood tinted to match the final color, countersink all exposed nailheads, sand again. Then you may reverently approach the manufacturer's can of paint. In the case of plaster walls, you must spackle. Preparing the spackle, you are told, requires a high degree of skill and

79

professional know-how. It fact, it is just like mixing batter.

I did not learn all this at once, because I didn't think it applied to me. My surfaces looked all right, so I simply painted—woodwork—as quickly as possible. I wanted to get it over with and go and sit in the sun. When I finished, there was paint on the floor, and I got up as much as possible, and some on the window panes, and I used a razor. What I couldn't get up, I stopped seeing—I had a splendidly accommodating eye. I looked at everything from a distance with a slight artistic squint, and it certainly seemed much fresher and brighter than before. I was pleased. It was almost creative.

I should never have assumed that one can ever get doing-it-yourself over with. Because people who had done it themselves began to come around and say things in level professional voices. They said, "You should work your paintbrush into the corners," and "When you paint a door, your strokes should not go every which way," and "Was your paint too thin? Enamel has a tendency to drip," and "I can't understand how you manage to get so much paint on yourself," and "I could give you a few tips on cutting edges," and finally they said, "And when are you going to do the second coat?"

My eyes stopped being accommodating. I saw dark corners, and drips, and sloppy edges, and my spatter-pattern loafers, and the room was no longer fresh and bright, but waiting for a second coat. "And you might have to do a third to cover up those brush strokes."

Thus it was that I learned to paint properly. Thus I discovered that I can do-it-myself, just like everyone else.

I won't.

It may be too late. Already, like everyone else who does it himself, I am beginning to be a fiend. Everywhere I go, no matter how hard I try to be a slob. I see drips and dark corners, my own and other people's. If I am not doing it myself physically, I do it mentally. My friends may think we are having an intellectual conversation, but I am repainting their woodwork. The paint is not going on well because they didn't clean the soot out of the corner, the slobs. After painting, I scrape and wax their floors, even when I have to use the kind of wax I don't like, which I saw in their kitchen.

I can't even read. In the first paragraph of *The Man in the Gray Flannel Suit*, there is a big dent in the plaster with a crack in the shape of a question mark leading out of it. They tried to fix it, but they must have done something wrong. I couldn't pay attention to the book, not to mention this delicate symbolism, until I had got out my trusty spackle and fixed the question mark.

Fiends are the apogee of the do-it-yourself movement. Most people have somebody to thank for something, but fiends have done everything all by themselves, including making themselves fiends. Their minds are cluttered up with all kinds of superior knowledge, and the minute they look at a wall, a floor, a piece of furniture, they take out their putty knife, and apply their knowledge with a wet smack.

With the prevalence of fiends, a moral shift has occurred. In the old days, a fiend might have been dismissed as "pison neat." In the old days, if your house was run down, it didn't necessarily mean you were a slob. Perhaps you didn't have the money to get it fixed.

Today fiends are respectable and there is no out for slobs. If you haven't got the money, you can do it yourself, and you can do it properly. When people arrive unexpectedly, you whisk out of sight, paintbrush in hand, and slip into your provincial swivel-top TV lounging outfit.

This is democracy gone too far. I refuse to work my fingers to the bone in order to look rich. And I have no chance to put the paintbrush in turpentine, so it dries up and gets stiff.

I am now defiending myself myself, because I get no help from anyone else. They continue to keep at me. "Make your home a show place—" "Reflect your good taste in—" "Know this—" "Do this—" "*Before* you do this—" "You can—"

They continue to assume that their time is worth more than mine. They think they are too busy to knock things up, but that I have all the time in the world. So they tell me it will be fun, and it will be good for me to do things with my hands, because it will take my mind off myself. I see no reason to take my mind off myself if all I do with it is put it on a do-it-yourself shelf.

There is no use their enjoining me any further. From now on I am going to have experts, big, serene, inarticulate experts, who know exactly what they are doing, and are unable to explain it to me.

I will be lying in the sun on a broken-down old beach chair, which I did not make myself, which is not a conversation piece, nor a handsome addition to my garden, nor scientifically designed, nor completely adjustable. All that it is is eminently and imminently collapsible. The expert will come and say, "It's the reverse rabbet in the china-closet screen that is the causing the trouble." I will not get

I Won't Do It Myself

up. I will not ask questions. I will say, "Let it out," and if I have any energy left after that, I will turn over slowly so as to get brown on the other side. And just in case, to be in the right position to see the reverse rabbet when it comes hopping backward out of the screen.

How I Am Never Going to Make Clam Chowder Again

The *Boston Cooking-School Cook Book* by Fannie Merritt Farmer is an institution, which means sophisticated people treat it tenderly, and unsophisticated people consider it a Bible. I would like Fannie Farmer to retire quietly and quickly. It is true that we are passing out of the era when she was *the* all-around cookbook, but she is still all around (in the drawer of the kitchen table) when you want a basic recipe, and still causing trouble.

Some of her recipes should be preserved as sociological curiosities. But not to eat—to be read. What she thought up! Canapés in particular excited her: she put oysters in a grapefruit. She also loved mock things—Mock Almonds, Mock Crabs, and Mock Cassava Bread, which most people would be unable to assess, never having eaten Real Cassava Bread. She created Cigarettes à la Prince Henry, made of puff paste and chicken forcemeat, and Lobster Boats, to which you add "sails made of rice paper and small wooden skewers, covering skewers with thin white cardboard." There is Peanut Salad, and a soup called Nymph Aurora, Halibut in Bed (in French), and Tournadoes of Beef, topped with a hominy-and-horse-radish croquette and a piece of banana.

In the more sober basic recipes, Fannie Farmer was unable to exercise her rich and untrammeled imagination. To be a New England institution, she had to include them, but I think that secretly she hated them. She wished to discourage everyone from making them, so that they would turn back to Nymph Aurora. So she set herself to making the basic recipes as complicated as possible. She played a game with herself to see if she could get every single utensil in the kitchen dirty.

In her recipe for New England Clam Chowder—I mean Clam Chowder—she comes closest to success. This is what happens:

Leaving out the list of ingredients, the recipe begins: "Clean and pick over clams, using one cup cold water; drain, reserve liquor, heat to boiling point, and strain." How do you pick over something with a cup of water? I couldn't imagine, so I put the clams in a saucepan, poured a cup of cold water over them, tossed them around a bit, and then emptied the whole business into a strainer over another saucepan. Then I saw that I was going to have to use the strainer again so I dumped the clams out of the strainer onto a chopping board. I heated the clam liquor to a boiling point and strained it into a third saucepan. For some reason I don't understand, one has to heat the clam liquor again later.

We have just begun, and we have used three saucepans, a measuring cup, a strainer, and a tablespoon to scrape out the clams. Total: six.

We continue: "Chop finely hard part of clams; cut pork in small pieces and try out; add onion, fry five minutes, and strain into a stewpan." One board and a knife for all the chopping. Trying out, according to Fannie Farmer, should be done in a double boiler, which adds two utensils, leaving out the cover. (I am still using the same tablespoon.) There is also the stewpan. The onion must be sliced, so what with that, chopping the salt pork, separating the hard and soft parts of the clams and chopping the former, and with potatoes coming up, one must use a second chopping board. With so many different little piles on one board, you risk losing one while you're scraping another (same dirty knife) into the pan. And I found the hard and soft parts of the clams difficult enough to keep straight, so I put what I thought was the soft part of the clams into a little bowl. Dirty utensils to date: thirteen.

I am mystified in this recipe as to why you strain the onion and salt pork. What Fannie Farmer wanted seems to have been fat slightly flavored with onion, so you are supposed to throw away the delicious golden brown onion and the crisp bits of fried salt pork. I couldn't bear to, so I put them aside in a separate dish to eat later. But since I was supposed to throw them away, it would be unfair for me to count this dish. I am attempting to be, not only fair, but as economical as possible throughout.

"Parboil potatoes [this is 4 cups of potatoes cut in ¾-inch cubes] five minutes in boiling water to cover; drain and put a layer in bottom of stewpan." The potato peeler is fourteen. In cutting up the potatoes I used the same knife and measuring cup. Saucepan to parboil potatoes is fifteen (fourth saucepan). You might use the same strainer to drain the potatoes, but if you drain them by the usual method of holding the lid a little askew and pouring the water out, you have another utensil, the lid of the pan. Total: sixteen.

Now you put a layer of potatoes in the bottom of the stewpan (still same tablespoon, somewhat gummy), add the chopped clams, sprinkle them with salt and pepper, and "dredge generously with flour." (Fannie Farmer loved to dredge with flour, which is what is wrong with her gravy.)

For this, I absolutely must have a clean spoon, since the other one has got potatoes and clams on it. Total: seventeen.

"Add remaining potatoes, again sprinkle with salt and pepper, dredge with flour." Pay close attention, because you didn't, in the previous paragraph, just sprinkle with any old amount of salt and pepper. You used 1 tablespoon of salt and ⅛ teaspoon of pepper, which means two more spoons. Since part goes in at one time, and part later, I also had to wipe off the table, because the remaining salt in the tablespoon fell out when I put it down to get the flour. I don't really blame that on Fannie Farmer. No, I couldn't use the same spoon I used for the flour, because I got mixed up and stirred with it, and now it is allover incipient clam chowder.

". . . and add two and one half cups boiling water." Same measuring cup, but I had to boil the water in something, and I had to boil it in something with a lid, because I am getting impatient. Total: twenty-one.

"Cook ten minutes, add milk." This is four cups of scalded milk. Here comes the measuring cup on its fourth sally (water, potatoes, water, milk). If you scald milk properly (page 27), you "heat over boiling water, covered, until milk around edge of pan has bead-like appearance." This means another double boiler, which is three more utensils, including the cover. I suppose I could use the same bottom and the same lid of the double boiler I used for trying out the pork, if I happened to have two double boilers exactly the same size. As it happens, I do, because the bottoms of double boilers have a tendency to boil away and get thrown out. But Fannie Farmer would never have let this happen, so, as far as she is concerned, the list of dirty utensils now stands at twenty-four.

"Add soft parts of clams, and butter" (four tablespoons recklessly measured with the salty tablespoon); "boil three minutes, and add crackers split and soaked in enough cold water to moisten." These should be "common crackers": I'm not sure what they are or why one must split them. But I did it with a clean knife. The old one had been used for pork, onion, potatoes, and for pushing things off boards into the stewpan. It was a mess. Parenthetically, it is typical of Fannie Farmer to soak something enough to moisten it. In any case, it involves a bowl and brings the total to: twenty-six.

I am not counting that I had to wipe off the clock on the dresser because I got butter and things on it when I turned it around to see when three minutes started.

"Reheat clam water" (all ready in saucepan Number 3) "to boiling point, and thicken with one tablespoon butter and flour cooked together." How do you do this? You use a fifth saucepan and another spoon. Total: twenty-eight.

It is finished, and the stewpan has a lid, so that makes twenty-nine.

I also have to wipe off the edge of the ruler I used to measure the ¾-inch cubes of potatoes. Thirty.

You may object that I could have boiled the water in the teakettle and that you don't have to wash the teakettle every time you use it. I did, but I did have to. The fat from the salt pork spattered on it because I didn't put a lid on the first double boiler. That was why I used a lid on the second one.

Thirty separate things to wash for one basic New England recipe is too institutional for me, and I don't feel tender about it. Take Fannie Farmer away and dredge her generously in flour to bury.

Too Many Cooks?

ONE OF THE REASONS I WRITE (YOU don't think I do it for fun, do you?) is because the human being in the twentieth century faces the terrifying fact that he is alone, alone, alone (I also do it for money). I speak to all of you across a void. Are you there on the other side? In a way, but from my point of view as likely as not you have little pointed heads and antennae and can't understand a word I am saying.

I want to communicate. I want to get across to you. The difficulties are, of course, created by me. The first one is that nothing that has happened to me has ever happened to any of you. I have had all these experiences for the very first time, and no amount of telling me different will convince me to the contrary.

The second is that when I am not with people I cease to exist for them. By this I mean that while I may talk about other people and other people may talk to me about other people, when I am not there no one ever talks about me.

I know, because people always suggest this sort of thing, that the only way I can get across to you, the only way I can believe that you're real and talking about me, is through an act of faith. I am therefore going to make a positive gesture in this direction and reveal something about myself. It is the most intimate and carefully guarded secret of all.

It must be, because none of you has ever admitted it to me. Either you are ashamed to admit it, or none of you has it.

I am ashamed to admit it, too, but I am going to. *I think about myself the whole time.* Even worse, I am not the only one doing it. There are at least four of us here.

I must say immediately that I have read the book called *The Three Faces of Eve*, which is about a lady who is two alternating and diametrically opposed personalities, then three, and finally a fourth. I have also read about Miss Beauchamp, in the earlier case history, *The Dissociation of a Personality*, by Morton Prince. In both these fascinating cases, when one personality takes over the others go away.

My case is even more fascinating, and quite different. No one of the various Sylvias can take over and blot out the others. They are all in there pitching every minute. No wonder I sometimes have dark circles under my eyes.

And how they do run on—talk, talk, talk, bicker, bicker, bicker. This is the third and most potent reason why it is hard for me to get across to the rest of you. How can I pay attention to what you're saying when I'm having such an absorbing conversation with myself?

To illustrate my case, I am going to give you an example of how we run on. Don't think I'm going to reveal any real secrets or low details. I am saving everything base for fiction, where I can pretend to be someone else—that is, a fifth or sixth person.

Serious students of human personality will find my account unscholarly. I offer it humbly on the chance that the untutored, *farouche* instinct of the creative artist will inadvertently disclose something they haven't thought of. (Who are you, calling yourself an artist? An artist is serious and disciplined.) There's one of them now. (I'm disciplined, too, but in a different way. Don't be pompous.) There's another.

I also realize that I am laying myself open to the charge of being utterly inconsequential in the thought processes. I am utterly inconsequential in my thought processes. The reason I'm writing this (now we are getting down to it) is in case there is someone around who is like me. Could it be that what I get from the rest of you is as carefully tailored and edited as what I give you? If so, let's all relax.

We are going to suppose that I am cooking up my usual delicious stew. Making stew provides everyone with exactly the right opportunity to engage in her customary squabble. You are getting two things for your money: a glimpse into the unknown depths of a human soul and a recipe for stew.

First you must buy a quantity of boneless chuck. I won't tell you any particular quantity. Unlike the cookbooks, I don't know how many people you are having for dinner.

SYLVIA NO. ONE (*We are listed in order of appearance*): The butcher likes me. He smiles and makes jokes. I'm less fussy and demanding than most women he waits on.

SYLVIA NO. TWO: Fussy! You're positively careless. You never bother to find out how much things are going to cost.

ONE (*Dreamily*): "She was so easygoing and open-hearted. Always a friendly word and a smile for everyone. We will all miss her now."

TWO: You're scared to be fussy because someone might be unpleasant to you. You're a coward.

ONE (*Taken aback*): Am I? Oh, dear. (*Thinks it over*) I am not. I rode the Cyclone at Coney Island.

TWO: You screamed the whole time.

ONE: So did you.

TWO: It was your fault. You made me go.

ONE: Anyway I enjoyed screaming, which is more than you did.

SYLVIA NO. THREE: Pay attention to what we're doing. We're *buying meat.*

The beef should be in rather large chunks.

ONE: How lavish and generous I am! Some people serve stew with little tiny bits of meat in it.

TWO: You had a lot left over the last time.

ONE: It was good, too.

THREE (*Firmly*): I would like to get this shopping over with. Shopping is boring.

ONE: Why, *I* don't think so. I am the type who finds possibilities of interest and enjoyment in everything. If I were a painter, that display of beans and lentils would inspire me into making a beautiful abstraction. And people's faces. How fascinating they are.

TWO: Look at that one. She hates me.

THREE (*To One*): Stop showing off. I am the type who pays attention to what she is doing. I am concentrated. When the rest of you leave me alone, I am.

We will now assume that we are all at home, with the shopping done and the groceries put away. We get out our frying pan.

ONE: Some people call it a spider. I wonder why. I think I'll look it up.

THREE: Don't try to do two things at once. We're *making stew.*

Brown the meat in butter in the frying pan.

THREE: It's burning!

SYLVIA NO. FOUR: I'm sorry. I just had to know. Originally frying pans had legs and were used over coals on the hearth. Get it?

THREE: Of course I do, but I'm not interested. You made me burn the meat.

TWO (*Wails*): It'll taste horrid!

FOUR (*Looks it over*): Don't be upset. It's not badly burned. It might improve the taste. Who knows?

Brown the meat in butter *if* you are feeling rich. It takes a lot.

ONE (*Musing*): "No matter what else she must skimp on, she always uses the best fresh butter, and a good wine."

TWO: How do you know it's a good wine? You have no palate. You'll drink anything. And everything.

ONE: Are you referring to last night?

TWO: When we were offered that highball after dinner, I was perfectly willing to wait awhile. But you had to have it.

FOUR: It tasted very good.

TWO (*To One*): I know what you think. You think if you drink enough, I'll go away.

ONE: You do, too. It's fun.

THREE: We have been through this before. I refuse to discuss which of you was responsible for that hangover. You all ought to know better.

TWO: I doubt if there is any good wine that costs a dollar and nine cents.

THREE: The wine will do *all right*.

FOUR: Let's try it, and see how it is.

THREE: Not right now. Put in some more meat.

FOUR (*Tasting it*): It's quite a nice wine.

TWO: Nice enough for stew. We shouldn't be extravagant.

THREE: I agree. I need new shoes.

ONE: Some one on the beach said my feet looked Greek. Do my hands look Greek, I wonder?

THREE: *Put in some more meat.*

TWO: They look bloody at present.

ONE: I wish there were someone around to read my palm. I love having my palm read.

THREE: I don't believe in that stuff.

TWO (*To One*): You like being the center of attention and having your hand held.

ONE: Yep.

TWO: That man who read our palm said I was inhibited. I am *not* inhibited.

ONE: On the contrary, I'm quite spontaneous.

THREE: I've watched you being spontaneous. My, you think you're good at it.

Having browned all the meat carefully on all sides, we take it out of the frying pan and put it into our earthenware casserole. Then we pour two or three tablespoonfuls of sherry over it (one of our secrets) and salt and pepper it. We start scraping the carrots and cutting them up.

ONE (*Sadly*): Carrots don't make your hair curl.

THREE: Like "kiss your elbow and you'll be a boy." When I was eight, I believed that. I tried and tried. I had read *Bob Graham at Sea* and I wanted to join the Merchant Marine.

ONE: I should put a little hand lotion on my elbows.

FOUR: It was that beautiful square-rigged training ship. I was dying to sail on it.

THREE: *Her.*

95

ONE: I certainly don't want to go into the Merchant Marine now. I'm perfectly satisfied with being a woman.

TWO: Are you sure?

FOUR: Yes. There are only one or two things I'd like to be clearer about.

ONE: Now I'm not even sure I'd like to go on a cruise with someone in a small sailboat. One is always tripping over cleats and ropes—

THREE: *Lines.*

ONE: —and cans of beans and oars.

TWO (*To Four*): Well, go on. What do you want to be clearer about? You should face your problems.

FOUR (*Distant*): I don't think I'm going to tell you right now. Things often solve themselves.

ONE: "As they tacked into the harbor, she was sitting on the gunwale, her long blond hair streaming behind her in the wind."

TWO: The damp sea breeze had taken every smitch of curl out of her long straight blond hair.

ONE: Making love in a bunk would be cramped.

FOUR: CENSORED (*She could manage it*)

TWO: You forget. She isn't in the bunk. She is still sitting in the gunwale. We just came about and she has been knocked overboard.

FOUR: Wonderful salt water. I love to swim.

TWO: If you'd give up smoking, you could swim much farther.

This goes along more quickly than it reads. We are now browning the carrots a little in the same spider, adding more butter if necessary.

TWO (*To One*): Stop pretending you're in that sailboat with

X. He hasn't given any indication that that's what he has in mind.

ONE: Do I need indications? He likes me.

THREE: You're quite mistaken. He likes *me*. Who sewed up his coat sleeve?

ONE: All right, whom did he recite that poem to?

TWO: He consulted me about his job.

FOUR: He knows I'm there. It's exciting.

SYLVIA NO. FIVE (*As much of a surprise to me as she is to you*): He does. And he suspects about me, which is more than the rest of you do. But I can wait. I'll come out the next time we see him.

We have dumped the carrots in the casserole, and are now peeling the onions, which should be the small white ones.

TWO: Do I cry more than most women?

ONE: You cried because you didn't think X liked you. It made me look awful. I could have killed you.

FOUR: There's a Picasso picture of a weeping woman, which looks the way I feel when I cry.

THREE: Does that make it good?

FOUR: I think so. If you were writing a review, you could phrase it more grandly.

ONE: Why, look at us! We made an artistic judgment while making stew. What a varied and interesting mind we have!

We brown the onions in the frying pan. Then we peel some mushrooms, depending on how big they are, cut them in quarters, and brown them. Here we really do have to add some more butter. Mushrooms sop it up. Dump these in the casserole, too. We are ready to make the gravy.

97

THREE: And please let's pay attention. I can't make a decent sauce with a quarter of our mind on it. Why can't I have some cooperation?

TWO: Stop scolding me. I always try to be good.

ONE: And how it bores me.

TWO: It's not my fault.

THREE: Stop it. Stir a little flour into the butter.

ONE: Not too much, or it won't taste French.

FOUR: A little tomato paste. That helps thicken it. And, if we have some, a little Bovril.

TWO (*Martyred*): I'm good for something. I didn't forget the Bovril.

ONE: "She is full of instinctive feminine wisdom. There is something French about her."

THREE: That's enough. It's all blended.

FOUR: Not quite. There's no hurry.

TWO: There is, too. Those people will be here in two hours. You know how I hate to be surprised.

FOUR: I love to be surprised.

ONE: *I* want you to hurry up, too. I have to have time to decide what to wear.

THREE: Now pour in the wine and scrape up all that brown stuff.

FOUR: Such a satisfactory way to get a frying pan clean.

ONE (*Still thinking about what to wear*): "A charming picture—no one would have guessed that a few moments before she had been bending over a hot stove."

TWO (*Disgusted*): Bending over a hot stove—what a cliché! At our age, you ought to be over that stuff. What about that aristocratic English family you used to be a member of every night before you went to sleep?

ONE: You're mean to bring that up. I forgot about them

long ago. (*Getting no sympathy at home, she addresses herself to a friend*) I am sorry to burden you with this information, but I have thought it over, and I know that in the end you would wish to have known. I have a fatal disease. I have only a year or two more. I hope to spend them well.

TWO (*Considering*): It would be pleasant. I would ignore all the people I don't like. I wouldn't write those letters. I wouldn't collect money for charity. I wouldn't do anything I didn't want to. Everyone would be nice to me.

THREE: No such luck. We'll all live to be eighty-five.

TWO (*Sighs*): I suppose so.

THREE: Now let's put in the beef bouillon.

TWO: If I were a really good cook, I'd have some beef stock made from scratch.

ONE: It takes a lot of time.

TWO: But it might be better to spend the time on improving myself. There's so much I haven't read—*The World of Mathematics*. Someone was talking about Balzac. I was ashamed I hadn't read anything of his.

FOUR: Were you? I wasn't.

TWO: I thought I should study French.

THREE: Salt and pepper.

ONE: A little thyme.

TWO: Bay leaf.

FOUR: How about a little oregano? We never tried oregano.

THREE: I wouldn't risk it.

But while she is talking, Four has put some in.

ONE: What do you think? Pretty good?

THREE (*Judiciously*): Just a little more salt.

They pour the sauce into the casserole, and turn on the gas under it.

THREE: A *low* flame. (*To Two*) If we organize our time properly, we should be able to do both. Now, if we can manage to get to bed every night by 11, up at 7—

FOUR: I think I'll read *The Red and the Black* next.

TWO: We should read *The World of Mathematics*. It's harder and it would be good for us.

FOUR: I'm sorry, but I want to read Stendhal.

THREE: We should set up some sort of criteria for ourself. The trouble with the modern world is that there are too many choices—

FOUR (*More or less to herself*): If I had more criteria, I might be leerier, but how much wearier to be superior. I'll be cheerier—

TWO: Stop being childish. This is not the moment for rhyming.

FOUR: I can rhyme while you get dressed.

THREE: Don't I know it. You're the one who sometimes has two cigarettes going in different ash trays.

ONE: No, she isn't. The other cigarette was mine.

FOUR: I'm so delighted these people are coming to dinner that I think I'll whip up a few criteria for dessert.

ONE: She is famous for her delicious criteria.

THREE: Her criteria are so professional that she could easily make her living if she were willing to sell them.

TWO: No matter what else she does badly, you can count on her criteria.

They laugh.

ONE: Look at us. We can be funny when we're all by ourself.

THREE: Stop looking at us. You do too much of that as it is.

Having finished the stew, they pause, wander around the room, and then all look at themselves in the mirror.

TWO: Why, oh why, is her nose so long?
ONE (*Tilting her head*): "You might say that she has moments of beauty. It is perhaps not so much her actual features as her expression—something dreamy, a little elusive—"
THREE (*Interrupting*): Color pretty good. No dark circles. Hair combed out all right. You'll pass.
FOUR: Is that you? So it is. Why does it go on and on being so surprising?

It is very good stew. Who, I (who?) wonder, made it?

III

Straying into the Library

The Death of Lady Mondegreen

WHEN I WAS A CHILD, MY MOTHER used to read aloud to me from Percy's *Reliques*. One of my favorite poems began, as I remember:

> Ye Highlands and ye Lowlands,
> Oh, where hae ye been?
> They hae slain the Earl Amurray,
> And Lady Mondegreen.

I saw it all clearly. The Earl had yellow curly hair and a yellow beard and of course wore a kilt. He was lying in a forest clearing with an arrow in his heart. Lady Mondegreen lay at his side, her long, dark-brown curls spread out over the moss. She wore a dark-green dress embroidered with light-green leaves outlined in gold. It had a low neck trimmed with white lace (Irish lace, I blieve). An arrow had pierced her throat. From it, blood trickled down over the lace. Sunlight coming through the leaves made dappled shadows on her cheeks and her closed eyelids. She was holding the Earl's hand.

It made me cry.

The poem went on to tell about the Earl Amurray. He was a braw gallant who did various things, including playing at the bar, which, I surmised, was something lawyers did in their unserious moments. (I grew up during prohibition, though I was against prohibition and for Governor

105

Smith.) The poem also said that he was the Queen's love, and that long would his lady look o'er the castle doun ere she saw the Earl Amurray come sounding through the toun. Nothing more was said about Lady Mondegreen.

But I didn't feel it was necessary. Everything had been said about Lady Mondegreen. The other ladies may have pretended they loved the Earl, but where were they? The Queen was probably sitting in Dunfermline toun drinking the blood-red wine along with the King (the one in "Sir Patrick Spens"). As for the Earl's wife, hiding in the castle in perfect safety and pretending to worry about him, it was clear she only married him so she could be Lady Amurray. She was such a sissy she probably didn't even look doun very hard—she was scared she'd fall through the crenelation of the battlements. As a matter of fact, she looked like a thin wispy girl I once socked in the stomach while I was guarding her in basketball because she kept pushing me over the line when the gym teacher couldn't see her and who was such a sissy that she fainted dead away so that everybody said I should learn to be a lady when really she was cheating—but I won't go into that. Lady Mondegreen loved the Earl truly, and she was very brave. When she heard that Huntly, the villain, was coming after him, she ran right out of her castle and into the forest to be with him without even stopping to change from her best dress.

By now, several of you more alert readers are jumping up and down in your impatience to interrupt and point out that, according to the poem, after they killed the Earl of Amurray, they *laid him on the green*. I know about this, but I won't give in to it. Leaving him to die all alone without even anyone to hold his hand—I won't have it.

The point about what I shall hereafter call mondegreens,

since no one else has thought up a word for them, is that they are better than the original.

Take Hizzeray. Hizzeray is that huge hairy muscular Etruscan in the *Lays of Ancient Rome* who was such a demon with the broadsword and who perpetrated one of the great betrayals of history. If Hizzeray had been there, Horatius couldn't have held the bridge a minute. Horatius was very brave, but Hizzeray was bigger. If not, why was he the first person Lars Porsena of Clusium thought of, when he swore by the Nine Gods that the great house of Tarquin should suffer wrong no more?

> And named a trysting-day,
> And bade his messengers ride forth
> East and west and south and north,
> To summon Hizzeray.

Hizzeray was hard to find or the messengers wouldn't have been told to go in so many directions, but he had no excuse. The messengers blew so many trumpets that tower and town and cottage heard the blast. I hoped Hizzeray would rush in at the last moment and knock Horatius into the Tiber. (I was on Lars Porsena of Clusium's side, though you're not supposed to be, because his name was so much better than anyone else's.) But Hizzeray never did. When they say

> Shame on the false Etruscan
> Who lingers in his home,
> When Porsena of Clusium
> Is on the march for Rome—

they mean Hizzeray.

Then there is Harold. You know Harold: "Our Father who art in heaven, Harold be Thy name." It's not one I would have picked myself, but if he has to have a name,

Harold will do. Harold has a tendency to corpulence: "O all ye works of the Lord; fleshy the Lord."

But he can do extraordinary things. There's a hymn which tells about it. As it is printed in the book, it says that he "moves in a mysterious way,/His wonders to perform." Actually, of course, what it says is that Harold "moves in a mysterious way—he wanders down a horn."

You must pray to Harold if you want something very specific. For instance, if you have discovered how very difficult it is to meet someone there, you say to Harold, "Lead us not into Penn Station." At the same time, Harold will protect you from those jittery, unreliable New York, New Haven, and Hotfoot trains. They aren't as dangerous when they're coming into nice motherly old Gran Central.

Even the mizz doesn't scare Harold. The mizz is a sort of elemental protoplasm, which looks like a thick, pulpy, shifting fog. It is inhabited by strangely shaped, white, squudgy animals, who moan quietly to themselves from time to time. The mizz is in the Evening Prayer Service: "Let the sea make a noise, and all that in the mizz."

If you decide that Harold is your shepherd, you can be sure of being looked after. If he can't be there himself, he will get in Good Mrs. Murphy and "Surely Good Mrs. Murphy shall follow me all the days of my life." I knew Mrs. Murphy, and I can't think of anyone I'd rather have follow me, though, knowing her, I think she would more likely be several blocks ahead. She could do almost as many things as Harold. She told fortunes in tea leaves, baked delicious bread in a frying pan, and once, when her little boy climbed onto the top of the roof and was too scared to get down, she shouted up to him, "You come right down, you little Irish basket," and like magic he got over being scared and came right down.

Mrs. Murphy lived in Massachusetts, where they have a holiday in April called Pay Treats Day. It always surprises and infuriates people who come from other states, because, just when they want to go out to buy shoes or bean pots, they find all the shops closed up tight, while the shopkeepers are out paying treats. This reminds me of Paul Revere, who rode to "spread the alarm through every middlesex, village, and farm." Middlesexes look a little like drumlins, if you know what they are, but they are made of hay, and so also look a little like haystacks. There is one middlesex exactly in between each village and farm. A person who is too poor to live in a village or farm lives in a middlesex.

And where the middlesexes, villages, and farms slope down to the sea, beyond the dunes, beyond the rocky coast, stands the Donzerly Light on a rugged, lonely promontory. At twilight, the lighthouse keeper turns it on, and it begins to spout rockets and bombs which light up the flagpole with the great big American flag which stands right next to it. This is where you go to pledge the legions to the flag.

There's a rude bridge around here somewhere, which is so dilapidated that it touches the flood.

There are many mondegreens which give fresh new insights into tired old ideas. With all due respect to Rudy Vallee, "I'm just a vagabond lover" seems a pretty wet notion nowadays. A friend of mine unwittingly sang it "I'm just a bag of unloving." If you've heard anything at all about psychiatry (who hasn't?) you will realize that a bag of unloving is a significant concept, and when you get a bag of unloving in search of a sweetheart, you've got the scheme of a well-developed neurosis, because as long as you don't have adequate feelings of self-esteem and love yourself, you can't love someone else.

One day I found, on the back page of the New York *Post*, a headline: GIANTS STRUGGLE UNDER WEIGHT OF 'DEAD' BATS. This is one of the most terrifying scenes I can think of, particularly since there seemed to be some doubt as to whether the bats are really dead. That would be bad enough, but if they were all stirring and squeaking—it would daunt even Hizzeray.

Then there are the people who, in between radio programs, sing a precise, cheerful, staccato little ditty that goes: "In just eight sec-onds, you get H-bomb." After I had counted eight seconds and hadn't got it, I came to enough to realize that they were continuing with "Gas and heartburn with Alkaid." So I began to wonder if some of them were singing "aid from" instead of "H-bomb" but at that point the announcer came on and said: "This is New York's fur station," and I knew there was a mondegreen influence loose in that studio.

And some years ago, before World War II, there was a quiet Sunday morning when I discovered that on the front page of the *New York Times* it said: 'WORLD BLOWS NEAR.' As I puzzled over this, I felt, in my room, the faint, fresh breath of the winds which were moving the turning world. Whose world was it? What was going to happen?

If you lay yourself open to mondegreens, you must be valiant. The world, blowing near, will assail you with a thousand bright and strange images. Nothing like them has ever been seen before, and who knows what lost and lovely things may not come streaming in with them? But there is always the possibility that they may engulf you and that you will go wandering down a horn into a mondegreen underworld from which you can never escape. If you want to be safe, guarded from the underworld and the creatures in the mizz, you have only to turn your back. And if you are this type of person, all you'll feel is a faint twinge of heart-burn over what you have missed—and you know how to get aid from that.

You have only to decide, as Humpty Dumpty put it (more or less), which is to be master, you or the word.

I am for the word, and against you.

Because there was a time, before she met the Earl Amurray, when Lady Mondegreen was a bag of unloving. Forlorn, in her embroidered dress, she looked out over her own crenelated battlement, wondering, all alone, about when the world would blow near so she could see what it was all about. Suddenly, beyond the moat, beyond the meadows, there is a stirring like dust far away on the horizon. A trumpet blasts, and she sees that it is the Earl Amurray, riding down the winding road, surrounded by men on prancing horses. Actually, they are Robin Hood's men, on a day off from Sherwood Forest, and the sun is glistening on their tunics of link and green. As the Earl Amurray spies Lady Mondegreen, he and his men spur their horses to a gallop and shout their wild, strange battle cry, "Haffely, Gaffely, Gaffely, Gonward." Lady Monde-green rushes down the long, winding stone stair. She reaches the portcullis and it rises as if by magic. The Earl Amurray seizes her, lifts her onto his horse, and they ride over the drawbridge together and out into the world.

At noon, they come to a babbling brook and they stop and tie their horse to a tree. Upstream a little way (here it is!) they see a rude bridge. The Earl Amurray pledges his legions to the flag to April's breeze unfurled and they go off, marching as to war, while the royal master leans against the phone, waiting for news of their victory.

Lady Mondegreen and the Earl Amurray are left alone by the brook. "Tell me," says Lady Mondegreen, as they sit down on the soft greensward in a crowd of gold and affodils, "Tell me" (for she is beginning to get a little bit hungry) "where is fancy bread?" And at this very moment, Good Mrs. Murphy, who has been riding a suitable distance behind on a sturdy mule, trots up and presents them with an Irish basket, which she has been carrying on her saddlebow. In it, wrapped in a damask napkin, is the fancy bread, a delicious small brown loaf, full of raisins and citron, and covered with white frosting.

After they have eaten, they wash their hands in the stream and rest awhile. Lady Mondegreen lies back on the grass and listens to the soft sounds of the mumblebees as they muzz among the affodils. The Earl Amurray entertains her by sounding through a tune in his fine baritone voice. Then they ride on. When night falls, they come at last to their own particular middlesex where they camp out under the stars, and Lady Mondegreen, because she loves him, does not say a word when the Earl takes all the covers.

Tragedy lies ahead and there is no one who can save them. Hizzeray is cowering in his home under a weight of dead bats. And alas, Harold, who has been watching them from above with a benign smile, cannot help. His horn has vanished, and there is no way he can wander down.

But even though the worst will happen, Lady Mondegreen and the Earl Amurray have had their journey together. Even if hereafter they get H-bomb, they have sniffed the delicate fragrance of the affodils, tasted the fancy bread, and slept together in the middlesex. Lady Mondegreen knows what the world is all about.

Lady Mondegreen is me.

Institute, Meet Artist

I HAVE BEEN READING THE ANNUAL REPORT of the Carnegie Corporation of New York, and a responsible and heartening report it is, such as one could normally file and forget. But one of the Carnegie Corporation's projects has fastened on my mind. The more I think about it, the more it fastens.

One of the most important obligations of the modern foundation, says the Corporation, is to foster creativity, "to discover and nurture gifted individuals." But what is this creativity? it asks itself. "What do we mean by a creative individual?" No one has pinned it down. The Corporation wants some "initial clarification of the problem."

To get some, it has made a grant of $150,000 to the University of California for a study of creativity. The study is to be carried out over a five-year period by the Institute of Personality Assessment and Research at Berkeley.

What a recondite and revolutionary institute! In my day, we had never heard of such a thing.

In my day at the University of California, no one asked me questions, assessed my personality, or measured my head. This may have been because my head was in a sunbonnet, and my connection with the University was parental. The University let me alone and I experimented: I ate a little dirt in the garden and recited poems to my doll. The dirt

113

was considered the problem, not the poems, though my mother, in between lecturing me about the dirt, wrote down the poems. I was illiterate at that period.

Things at Berkeley must have come a long way. Nowadays they undoubtedly measure the professors' children's heads, the amount of dirt they eat per day, and their poems.

Now that it has been established that creativity is a problem, how is the Institute going to attack it? Presumably it will collect some creative personalities and study them to see how they got that way and what it's like. (It mustn't let Painter A and Writer B see each other passing in the hall. If it does, neither of them will think the Institute has any discrimination.)

But this would mean that the Institute can already tell which personalities are creative and which aren't. If it can, it certainly wouldn't need $150,000 and five years. It would need a week or so at a smaller figure to write down how it knows.

So that can't be it. I'm sure the Institute is much too scholarly to leap to untested conclusions about who is and who isn't creative.

Yet it will have to get some creative personalities somehow. Suppose it decides to collect a few who are generally accepted by the world at large to be creative. Igor Stravinsky, for instance, lives right down the state a way and might be willing to come up and have his head measured. Of course the Institute should pay his expenses.

At this point, someone in the Institute will point out that Henry Miller—just for instance—is nearer, and would therefore be cheaper. Unless it has money enough for both (and what about Groucho Marx?—he's in California, too) the Institute will have a fight on its hands.

I don't think this can be the method either. If the Institute is scholarly, it is not going to accept a mass opinion. It will have to have a better basis than that for its value judgments.

I'm glad this method is ruled out, because, although it is none of my business, I don't want the Institute taking up too much of Stravinsky's time. I would like it better if they used the money to send Stravinsky something very nice—say, a case of fine brandy—and let him get on with whatever he's doing in a mellow glow.

So it must be that the Institute will take a middle ground: it will use, not its own judgment or the public's, but that of authorities, the critics and scholars specializing in the various arts and sciences. How is it going to establish that they are authorities? I don't know. It looks as if it will have to take their word for it, or else check every authority with all the others and see which gets the most votes. That would be the democratic procedure.

Something has just occurred to me. I have been assuming that the Institute is interested, not in people who might create, or in people who do create, but in people who create well. But how can it limit itself like that? The study won't be authoritative unless a good creator is compared both with a bad and with an unrealized one. The Institute is going to have to assess exactly three times as many personalities as I had originally thought.

I don't envy the Institute this situation. With so many people around, how can they keep them separated? I can see them milling around in the halls, having coffee together, comparing notes on the questions they have been asked, and drawing conclusions. Eventually everyone's category will get out, and there will be accusations, recriminations, and, almost certainly, tears.

And this is only the beginning of the Institute's job. It can't confine itself to living creativity alone. For all we and it know, living creativity is quite different from dead creativity. Many things could make it so—atomic fallout, frozen foods, Freud, or the fact that it isn't dead yet. To have a controlled study, the Institute will have to study dead creativity also.

It is going to have to read and study things like Beethoven's sketchbooks, Flaubert's letters, Van Gogh's letters, Joyce Cary's *The Horse's Mouth*, the Modern Poetry Collection at the Lockwood Memorial Library of the University of Buffalo, and hundreds of others. Undoubtedly the Institute already has a little man with a Ph. D. put away in a special room to do so.

If it doesn't, and if it should happen to read this, there is a great deal I haven't read yet, and I'd like to visit California, and $150,000 is a lot of money, and I would be willing to go out and do some reading for a minimal sum if my expenses were paid.

But it dawns on me that I am already there. I have been puzzling so over how the Institute will operate, and feeling so sorry for it, that suddenly I know what is going to happen. I can see it.

The scene is Institute's office. Institute has given Artist some tests, and now wants to talk to him, as Institute to Artist, about his working habits and sources of inspiration.

The Institute is considerate, so it has scheduled its interview in the later afternoon in order not to interrupt Artist's working day. I see Artist as a musician, because painters don't like to talk much, and writers talk too much, in addition to having an occupational tendency to tell lies.

INSTITUTE: Good afternoon, Artist. Did you have a good day?

ARTIST: It's raining. I must do something about my shoes.

INSTITUTE (*Brightly*): This is the rainy season here. I was referring to your work. How did it go?

ARTIST: These are pretty good shoes. Do you like them? Can I have that newspaper? (*Artist takes off shoes, stuffs them with newspaper, and places them side by side behind him.*) That's the best thing to do with shoes when they're wet. (*Artist sits back and crosses his feet, revealing a small hole in the toe of his sock. He studies it with interest*) Can you darn socks?

INSTITUTE (*Hesitates, then remembers that first things come first*): How did your work go today?

ARTIST: Fine. What do you know about these Carnegie people? The thing is this: If I could get a thousand dollars I could finish my symphony. Let me think. I can live on two hundred a month. Say fifteen hundred. That would cover copying too.

INSTITUTE (*Gentle but firm*): I am afraid our research project cannot handle this type of request. I can refer you to someone who will direct it through the proper channels.

ARTIST: That sounds slow. There must be a quicker way. I could marry a beautiful girl, who is also rich. Are you married?

INSTITUTE: Did you begin work right after breakfast?

ARTIST: A beautiful girl who is in love with me and whom I am in love with. Breakfast? You know, your oranges here aren't as good as I've always heard. Florida oranges have more taste. And Italian oranges—(*Artist begins to dream*)—the best in the world. I'll tell you what I'd have if I were in Rome now. First, melon with prosciutto. Then fettucine. Then a steak with a big salad. Chianti Brolio. (*With surprise and delight*) I'm hungry.

INSTITUTE (*Indulgent*): That sounds like a wonderful dinner.

ARTIST: That was lunch. For dinner, I'd start with artichokes—

INSTITUTE (*This could go on indefinitely*): Let's discuss what you did today.

ARTIST: Don't you like to talk about food? I do. Today—(*Artist looks sad*) I had a hamburger.

INSTITUTE: And after lunch, you went back to work?

ARTIST: I read Shakespeare and then I took a nap.

INSTITUTE (*Taking out notebook*): Shakespeare? That's interesting.

ARTIST: Don't you read Shakespeare?

INSTITUTE: I have a good many technical journals to keep up with. Does Shakespeare inspire you?

ARTIST: I like to read him. I'm trying to understand Sonnet a hundred and twenty-nine. What do you think it means? It's the one that begins—

INSTITUTE: I'm afraid I haven't read it very recently.

ARTIST: Oh. Is there any place I can go swimming around here? I'd like to get some exercise. (*Looks quizzically at Institute*) I should get in condition for the California girls.

INSTITUTE (*Coldly*): The Recreation Office[1] can give you information on the local beaches. What else do you read?

ARTIST: The sports page. There's a good fight tonight.

INSTITUTE: I don't know much about prize fighting.

ARTIST: Want to go? I'll take you. Let's go and have a

---

[1] The Institute will need an office like this.

drink now. You can go on interviewing me. We'll have very dry Martinis.

INSTITUTE (*Tries to remember if she was supposed to study the relation of creativity to alcohol*): I'm afraid that's impossible. Uh, does it help you creatively to drink?

ARTIST: I like a drink at the end of the day.

INSTITUTE: You feel pretty tired at the end of the day?

ARTIST: Tired? Do I look tired? (*Gets up and looks in mirror*) I don't look too tired. Hmmmm. (*Straightens tie*) I look pretty good. (*Turns and looks Institute over*) How old are you?

INSTITUTE: If you are wondering if I am qualified to conduct this interview, I have my Ph.D. in Personality. I wrote my thesis on "Some Aspects of Measurement in the Judgment of the Kleinkopf Test."

ARTIST (*Impressed*): That sounds learned. Which is the Kleinkopf Test? The one with the ink blots, or the one with the dirty pictures?

INSTITUTE: The Kleinkopf Test is the one with the paper dolls.

ARTIST (*Damped*): I didn't do so well on that one. I didn't intend to cut off that doll's head.

INSTITUTE (*Consoling*): We recognize that a creative personality is not necessarily gifted with manual dexterity.

ARTIST: Listen, that test with the pictures is very poor. You should change it.

INSTITUTE (*Her bailiwick*): The Thematic-Apperception Test has been used for many years, and is extremely valuable.

ARTIST: The pictures are badly drawn.

INSTITUTE: That has nothing to do with the value of the test.

ARTIST: It had a lot to do with the way I reacted. Isn't that important?

119

INSTITUTE: I don't believe you understand the purpose of the test.

ARTIST (*Suspiciously*): How did Stone do on the paper dolls?

INSTITUTE: I am not permitted to give information about the tests of the other creative personalities.

ARTIST: I don't care how good he was with the paper dolls. He can't play the piano. Asparagus fingers!

INSTITUTE (*Interested—this is one of the areas of investigation*): You do not find Stone creative?

ARTIST: Creative? He's a schmoe.

INSTITUTE: Could you elaborate that?

ARTIST: No.

INSTITUTE: Let's talk about your working habits.

ARTIST: I don't have any habits. I just go to work.

INSTITUTE: How do you put yourself into a creative mood?

ARTIST: How do you put yourself into a mood to judge Kleinkopf Tests?

INSTITUTE: I don't. I just do them.

ARTIST: That's what I do.

INSTITUTE: Surely you recognize that there is a qualitative difference between judging Kleinkopf Tests and writing music. I don't need inspiration to judge Kleinkopf Tests.

ARTIST: Don't you like your work?

INSTITUTE: Some of it's dull.

ARTIST: Look at the opportunity you have—$150,000! Nobody in the past had such facilities. Think of what you could find out. I'd be interested in knowing—

INSTITUTE: We are investigating your work.

ARTIST: I told you. I'm writing a symphony.

INSTITUTE: Could you describe in more detail exactly what you are doing?

ARTIST: (*Thinks*): Do you know what double counterpoint is?

INSTITUTE: More or less.

ARTIST: What do you mean—more or less? Either you do or you don't. Do you know what development is?

INSTITUTE: Well—

ARTIST: Polytonality?

INSTITUTE: Not exactly.

ARTIST: Cancrizans canon?

INSTITUTE: No.

ARTIST: Then how can I tell you what I'm doing?

INSTITUTE: You can try.

ARTIST (*Looks plaintively at Institute*): I'm sorry. (*Thinks*) Practice. You study the great composers. Technique. It's all in the technique. Some things come. (*Looks at Institute*) A great deal has been written about this. I could give you some things to read. There's a letter of Mozart's, for example—

INSTITUTE: But I'm supposed to investigate you.

ARTIST: Mozart describes it better. All right, ask me some more questions.

INSTITUTE: What were your feelings today while you were working?

ARTIST: Feelings? It's going good. I have a little theme like this—po, po, po, on the oboe. I'm sorry. I can't sing. (*Happily*) I worked six hours today. (*Artist gets up and stretches*) *I feel great.* (*Wanders around the room while Institute quickly writes in notebook. Artist watches Institute*) You didn't tell me if you were married?

INSTITUTE: I'm not.

121

ARTIST: Are you in love?

INSTITUTE: You shouldn't ask impertinent questions.

ARTIST (*Pleased*): I like you when you're mad. Why shouldn't I ask questions? I'm interested. You ask me questions.

INSTITUTE: My questions are scientific. Stop prowling around in your stocking feet.

ARTIST: If I put my shoes on, will you come and have a drink with me?

INSTITUTE: No.

ARTIST (*His tone would move mountains*): Oh, come and have a drink. There are lots of things you haven't found out about me. I'll be very nice to you. I'll give you a good dinner. I'll tell you all the right questions to ask. Then we can go back to my place, and I'll—

INSTITUTE: I don't think I should.

ARTIST: I was going to say that I'd play the piano for you.

INSTITUTE: Oh.

ARTIST: Disappointed?

INSTITUTE: Certainly not.

ARTIST: I guess I'd better be going. What's the name of the girl who does the ink blots? She'll go out with me.

INSTITUTE: She probably will. She'd go out with anybody.

ARTIST: I was good at the ink blots. She helped me.

INSTITUTE (*Stiffly*): It is not a test for proficiency.

ARTIST: She has beautiful blue eyes.

INSTITUTE: And a double chin.

ARTIST: I like you better.

INSTITUTE (*Off guard*): Do you?

ARTIST: If you're good, and come and have a drink with me.

INSTITUTE: You're impossible.

ARTIST: What kind of a value judgment is that?

INSTITUTE (*Laughs*)

ARTIST: Now we're in business. Come along. You want to foster creativity, don't you? That's what the Institute is for, isn't it? The way to foster creativity is to make me feel good.

INSTITUTE: !

ARTIST: Okay, I'll put my shoes on. By the way, can you darn socks?

What Was Good Enough for Mr. Rochester

DESCRIPTIONS IN BOOKS ARE A PROB-
lem to me, because I have only one living room. It is a long
room, running north and south. I am south, standing between two windows which look on the road—or driveway,
depending on how rich we are—at the front of the house.
In the middle of the wall on my left is the door into the
hall—a great hall with a curving staircase, or just a hall
with a staircase, depending on how rich we are. (If you are
like me, your mind has already begun to wander. One reason I have only one living room is that I find it hard to pay
attention to descriptions.) In the center of the right-hand
wall is a fireplace and, beyond, a door opening into the
garden. Opposite me, on the north wall, is the door into the
dining room—or an archway, if we are in *Jane Eyre*. (I'm
sorry, but these details are necessary.)

The sofa is to the left of the fireplace, and it is here that
Mr. Rochester lies with his foot on a cushion, while he
looks at Jane Eyre's mournful water colors. There are
"beautiful books and ornaments on the consoles and chiffonières." After his dinner party, Mr. Rochester, standing
by the piano, sings in his "mellow powerful bass" to Miss
Ingram's accompaniment, while Jane Eyre sits in the window seat, half hidden by the curtains, making a net purse.
The window seat is under the windows at the south end of
the room. I am always south.

Take out Mr. Rochester. Countess Rostov, feeling weary, sits on the sofa, receiving guests on her name day, and Natasha runs in from the hall, giggling over her doll.

Move the room part-way across Moscow, and Pierre is startling the guests at Anna Pavlovna's soiree by defending Napoleon.

To the right of the door into the hall is a large desk. Here Mr. Darcy writes a letter to his sister, while Miss Bingley admires his speed in writing and Elizabeth Bennet watches. My impression is that I am—I mean Elizabeth Bennet is— sitting on the window seat in the south window.

To the left of the door into the hall is the grand piano, with its keyboard in the middle of the room. Elsie Dinsmore sits on the piano stool. She is refusing to play the piano because it is the Sabbath, and her father has said she must sit there until she obeys him. (I have already solved this problem by playing "He Who Would Valiant Be," so I am sitting all alone in the window seat, watching, and I am annoyed.) Presently, Elsie Dinsmore faints, and Mr. Travilla says, "Dinsmore, you're a brute!"

Mme. Bovary has just bought two large blue glass vases for the mantelpiece, and the men from Rumpelmayer's will soon be here to take the doors off the hinges for Mrs. Dalloway's party.

Books where things don't happen in the living room make me nervous. For example, near the beginning of *A Handful of Dust*, there appears the troubling phrase: "the shuttered drawing room." Things take place in the morning room, but I am not comfortable in morning rooms and libraries. To get through *A Handful of Dust*, I had to go into the drawing room, open the shutters, throw open the windows—the room needed airing—take the dust sheets off the furniture, and, ignoring Mr. Waugh, push Tony, Brenda, Mr. Beaver, and the Princess Abdul Akbar into the room. Then we could get going.

The furnishings of my living room are flexible. If Beth March toasts bread on a toasting fork over the coals, I tuft the sofa to match. When we are at Thrushcross Grange, I carpet the room with crimson, and install a chandelier which shimmers with little soft tapers. Cathy and Heathcliff are peering in the window. When I get to Howard's End, I put a sword over the mantelpiece for Charles Wilcox to kill Leonard Bast with. For Mr. Rochester I make the mantelpiece marble, and the fire is a coal fire. When Nancy Mitford's Uncle Matthew appears, I hastily shift it to a wood fire, with plenty of ashes because he gets up very early in the morning to catch the maids before they take them out. He is quite right.

Authors are bad about picking up after themselves. English families always leave things around, copies of the *Tatler* and *Sketch* on the tables, riding crops or gloves on the chimney piece (Uncle Matthew, now that he's come in, doesn't think nice people say "mantelpiece"). These have to be removed before a Russian or American family moves in. The morning after one of Gatsby's parties, there are rings from glasses on all the consoles and chiffonières. I have Jeeves take them off with a little salt and oil mixed, before the Duchess of Wrexe arrives. She would not approve.

Carol Kennicott is a nuisance, because she redecorates. She takes out the golden-oak table with brass knobs, the moldy brocade chairs, and the picture of "The Doctor." It doesn't occur to her that I have to move them in first. But I help her bring in a new broad sofa with pillows of sapphire velvet with gold bands, though, left to myself, I would omit the gold bands. What really disturbs me is that, in the course of the redecoration, someone says there is no fireplace. This is out of the question, so I compromise by making it a gas log to go with the town of Gopher Prairie.

For *Moths*, by Ouida, I have to make the whole room white, and bring in "banks and pyramids of rose-hued azaleas," as the only touch of color. Now we are in Prince Zouroff's drawing room at Villafranca, where Corrèze, the famous tenor who is also a marquis and who loves the beautiful and saintly Vere, Princess Zouroff, sings some verses of Sully Prudhomme which insult Prince Zouroff, a brute who is being unfaithful with a quadroon called Casse-une-Croûte. Honest. Princess Zouroff is wearing white velvet, with a knot of white lilac at her breast, her only ornament the great pearls, and so on. I've gone into detail, because no one but me has read *Moths*. It is well worth doing over the living room for, although I cringe every time I paint the piano white. I doubt if it's good for it.

So, on the whole, my room is serviceable, and, except in unusual cases like the above, the furniture remains much the same, of a period one might call literary nondescript. Authors are not much interested in furniture. And frequently I have tenants like Archibald Marshall's Squire, who says that what was good enough for his father is good enough for him, so Mrs. Clinton doesn't dare change anything.

But, for no reason that I can explain satisfactorily or psychiatrically, certain things cannot be altered. One, as I have mentioned, is the fireplace. Another is the position of the piano. If an author puts the piano in the diagonally opposite, or northeast corner, I try to cooperate. I block up the door into the garden, and put a window there instead.

I stop myself from putting a radiator under the window, because that would be bad for the piano. But while I'm doing this, the piano scoots across the room, swivels around—scuffing up rugs in the process—and fits itself into its original corner. I push it back, suppress the radiator again, and put blocks in front of the piano's feet, to keep it in place. It pushes the blocks in front of it and moves right back to where it originally was, slowly.

The intransigence of my piano makes getting in a second one very difficult. A great-aunt of mine wrote a book in which she described studying with Liszt in Weimar. My great-aunt and Liszt were banging away happily (four hands) in my living room, when she startled me by mentioning an occasion when Liszt sat down and accompanied her in a Rubinstein concerto at a *second* piano. I knew I couldn't turn my piano around, so I had to yank it out into the room, and quickly stick another (going the other way) in behind it, so the first one couldn't roll back into the corner.

Certain books are pre-living-room, and for these I have a modification of my living room. It is a baronial hall, with a high ceiling with smoked-up rafters. At the north end is a dais, with a dinner table for important people, like Cedric the Saxon and Rowena. On the east wall is the fireplace—a huge one with suckling pigs on spits. In the middle of the room is a large table for serfs, and the door into the hall (or courtyard) is in the usual position on the west wall.

I use the baronial hall for fairy stories, for historical and mythical works, for taverns (with several small tables instead of one big one), and for Islandian interiors. I also use it for the *Odyssey*, with Penelope's loom on the dais, and the suitors sitting around in the middle of the hall.

Homer is easy to visualize because, unlike most authors,

he is orderly. His characters always put their spears away in a well-worn rack. Eurycleia hangs up Telemachus' tunic on a peg. Odysseus' bow is kept in a case, also hung on a peg. Homer makes it clear what he thinks of the suitors, by describing them many times as throwing their cloaks down on chairs.

He also has a feeling for comfort. I know no other author who always puts a rack for the feet on his chairs. I would like to give one of these chairs to Countess Rostov.

Recently when I read Robert Graves's *Homer's Daughter*, I was happy to find I could use the same hall with the same furnishings. Mr. Graves believes the *Odyssey* was written by a woman, possibly because of Homer's neatness. I think Mr. Graves is wrong: neatness is not a feminine, but an epic, quality. This means it takes time. In his short, modern book, Mr. Graves cannot be as neat as Homer. He leaves some purple covers soaking in a trough, and I think they have mildewed and run. Homer would have taken them out, dried them in the sun, and put them away in a well-made chest.

The one knotty problem in the *Odyssey* is Odysseus' bed. I must explain that, for ordinary circumstances, I have two bedrooms. One is a very small hall bedroom, containing a bed, a chest of drawers, and a desk. I use it for squalid and poverty-stricken scenes, and, a little cleaned up, for struggling young geniuses in big cities. Raskolnikov lives here, and it is also here that, after stooping to folly with the young man carbuncular, I smooth my hair with automatic hand and put a record on the gramophone. The gramophone is on the desk.

My other bedroom is very large, with a double four-post bed, and a luxurious dressing table with silver toilet articles. When I am sitting at the dressing table, brushing my hair, His Lordship looks at me in the mirror over my bare shoulder. Next to this bedroom is a dressing room where His Lordship sleeps when we are having a fight.

Odysseus' bed is too big for the hall bedroom. One of the bedposts of Odysseus' bed is an olive tree, in girth much like a pillar, which he built the bed around. He cut off the top, and smoothed the sides with an ax. I tried this bed in my large luxurious bedroom, and for a while it was fine. Then in the middle of Penelope and Odysseus in bed telling each other about everything, I realized that the trunk of the olive tree must come right up through the living room which is on the floor below.

Now, I do have a version of my baronial hall which has a tree in it. This, of course, is Hunding's hall, and the tree is Der Esche Stamm (or the Branstock, if we are in the Norse instead of the Wagnerian version). This tree is for gods with nothing better to do to thrust swords into. But it is too much for me to turn Der Esche Stamm into an olive tree and get it up through the ceiling onto the second floor, and what would I do with the room below afterwards? Odysseus' bedroom has got to be on the ground floor, and this is how I realized that Ithacans lived in bungalows. I don't like it, because for me things don't happen in bungalows.

Besides, Odysseus' bed sprouts every spring, and I have to keep cutting off the top with an ax. Still one must expect to have to take a certain amount of trouble if one reads the classics.

Only very secure readers can afford to have a great many rooms. I keep mine to a minimum because I'm afraid not to. I don't like rooms to get out of control. In Kafka's *The Trial*, the room which leads to the Interrogation Chamber is empty except for a washtub, but when K. returns it is a completely furnished living room. This almost threw me, but I managed it. (I put a screen around the washtub.) Poe did let a room get out of control, and the results were bad. Rooms are alive in a different way than we are, but their life is just barely conceivable, like that on Mars, where canals dig themselves while whistling airless be-bop between their long white teeth if I don't watch myself. Suppose I let Raskolnikov have a room for his very own? When I open the door I may find him playing Liszt's "Totentanz" on two binaural gramophones, while a chair with a rest for the feet dances with a white grand piano. I can't chance this kind of thing. I mean to lead a long, healthy life and continue to read books with rooms and not lower my guard for a minute.

Titles on the Loose

A TITLE IS A DELICATE THING. YOU DO not work on it. Either it is elusive, and you continue to cast a net until you catch it, or it is there, and you recognize it. Trapping titles is a high point of the writer's art, so naturally enough editors always want to change them. Editors don't catch titles: they think them up. When an editor sees an author's title, his pencil itches. It's not a question of the editor's title being better. It's a question of its being different.

This is not a pedestrian-versus-motorist complaint. I have been both, and when I was an editor I thought up some brilliant titles. Inevitably, the stiff-necked writer yelled murder. He was suffering from the mistaken notion that what he had produced was his.

Yet the writer has a consolation, as private as a vice. These are the beautiful titles which appear from nowhere, but which never achieve stones. Sometimes they are so compelling that one struggles for a long time to create tails for these kites. Eventually one must become reconciled to the fact that their being is as unique and fugitive as that of a mule. They are dubious in ancestry and barren of descendants.

I have several such titles, and all of them are more weighted with significance and suggestiveness than many pieces of writing I have struggled over. One of them is "Stop

133

Moving Pianos in My Dreams." It was, of course, a real dream, and a tiring one, and I am not interested in any amateur psychoanalysis on the subject. It is possible that it is meant for the refrain of a song. I mention this because my cooler judgment tells me that it is somewhat comical ("You may cut my rugs. You may shake my beams. But STOP . . . etc."). But its true quality for me is not comical. It is the ultimate in renunciation. It represents the finality of a decision made after long stress and strain, when some outrageous act has precipitated a total break. It is the worm turning. It is calling a halt. Stop moving pianos in my dreams.

On another level is a title that eats at me because I cannot place it: "When Creek Meets Creek." Is it profound or frivolous? Creek meeting creek is infinitely poetical, and the creeks could symbolize two people. But these people are Indians. Why does this make it funny? Am I anti-Creek? This one harasses me. I will give it away to anyone who can use it.

I am much clearer about the unfulfilled purpose of my next title. A few years ago I was engaged in clearing out a family house in Cambridge, Massachusetts. The house was being sold to the Mormon Church, which was forming a center there. I resented my occupation: as everyone knows who has done it, it is physically tiring and spiritually dispiriting to dismantle another generation. I had nothing against the Mormons, who were good, pleasant, and extremely respectable, except that, as good people can, they made me feel raffish. When they came to see me and to measure things, I knew they were quite tolerant about the fact that they often found me drinking coffee or smoking a cigarette. Did they see the *bottles* on the sideboard? It

134   *Titles on the Loose*

was something evil in me that made me wander around our house in my blue jeans, dropping cigarette ash into the debris of the past, and muttering to myself, "How Latter Day Can You Get?"

In its brash disdain, this is a magnificent title, but where can I use it? I am not equipped to write an article about Mormonism, and I don't particularly want to. If I did, the editor would change my title to "Whither Mormonism?"

". . . can you get?" is fashionable at the moment, and is used in the subtitle of another title I like. This one was a reaction to one of those articles by psychiatrists, which interprets your neurosis by how you furnish your apartment. The author believed that one expressed one's own uncertainties, etc., in the furniture one chose. "Breasts," he said, "or the lack of them, are frequently a matter of concern. . . . Breast imagery is indicated in a certain bloated kind of upholstery."

I resented this article because I felt (see above) that I had had little choice in the matter of furniture. All my furniture comes from the old homestead, so it says nothing about me except that I do, too. A lot of it belonged to my grandmother, and is bloated. She was not. So the title of the article I knew I was never going to write in rebuttal was "Leave My Grandmother's Breasts Out of This," or "How Tufted Can You Get?"

A title with a colon is particularly portentous. I have always wanted one. I thought one up once, which to me had everything: solemnity, provocativeness, optimism, and colon. It was "Compulsive Sloth: New Hope for the Perplexed." The article attached to this title went to a woman's magazine, and the editors, lively ladies with itchy pencils, promptly changed it (as you have seen elsewhere) to "What Have I Been Doing All This Time?" This is a nice title, too. If they had called my attention to it, I might have written another article to go with it. Now I can't. Nor can I use "Compulsive Sloth: New Hope for the Perplexed" for something else. It's too bad, but editors have no instinct for economy with writers' property.

One title haunts me more than the others. It occurred when, in a noisy restaurant, a friend told me about a book he had read and admired. I thought I heard him say that it was called *The Gobi Twin*. By the time we got it straight, and I was promising to look up *The Go-between* by L. P. Hartley, I was well along with *The Gobi Twin* by Sylvia Wright.

Gobi Twinship is a relationship that has never before been named, and I don't yet know its full implications. It may be feeling like a Siamese Twin while being separated from someone by a desert. It may be feeling like a twin while a desert opens in one's heart. Or it may be the relationship between two Mongolian idiots, who, against all odds, stick to each other through thick and thin on a high windy plateau. It may be all of these, and something more. Somewhere there is a person whose Gobi Twin I am, and when I find him, I will know all. I will write the book. Then an editor will brood and itch, pencil in hand, until, with a murmur of satisfied triumph, he will change the title to—*Time for Love?*

Me as White Goddess

HERE WE ARE IN A WORLD OF COMpromise, cooperation, counseling, conformity, togetherness and altogetherness. Here we are, trying to be civic-minded, open-minded, group-adjusted, and regularly dusted.

What a delight in this world to come upon Mr. Robert Graves, who has offered me the entrancing possibility of being the White Goddess.

Mr. Graves offers his theory about the White Goddess in the book of the same name. He elaborates it, with myths, charms, riddles, tree alphabets, spiral castles, roebucks in thickets, and other captivating devices, into 392 pages. I mention this because when I summarize his theory in a few paragraphs I will be unfair.

On first acquaintance, the theory is complicated, fantastic, but heady.

The White Goddess is, for one thing, the Muse. Male poets are supposed to invoke the Muse, to be inspired by her, to describe her, and to elaborate on their relationship with her, which will supply them with ample authentic poetic subject matter. Male poets also always lose the Muse, which supplies them with ample authentic subject matter for poems about being unrequited.

To explain why they always lose the Muse, one must go back to the time when history was mythology, except that

Mr. Graves contends that mythology is history. In this misty and distant period of what I shall hereafter call mythtory, society was matrilineal. There were no fathers, or no one knew who they were. Women were top dog and everyone worshiped the White Goddess.

Depending on where you lived, you might worship her as a mare, sow, or cow goddess. In various shapes, she was all over the ancient world, usually also in folds, sometimes three, sometimes nine. In three, she was bride, mother, and old woman. In nine, she gets divided up again in terms of sky, earth, and underworld, and under these in the following subheads: new moon, full moon, waning moon; spring, summer, winter; birth, procreation, death. She covers almost all the territory there is (by night light), and a good deal of poetic subject matter.

On second acquaintance, one finds this theory fantastic, heady, and exerting a strange fascination. The White Goddess sounds as if she had a fine time.

Mr. Graves says she is most poetically potent as a moon goddess. In this guise, she regularly takes as her lover the God of the Waxing Year. Eventually (six months later, I assume), he is killed by the God of the Waning Year, who in turn becomes the goddess's lover. This keeps up indefinitely. By a method I have not quite mastered, which involves her swallowing a bean or something of the sort, one of these gods is her son by the other.

On third acquaintance, I wonder if the White Goddess has as good a time as an ordinary woman.

The poet, says Mr. Graves, identifies himself with the God of the Waxing Year. Thus he inevitably gets it in the neck, and this is good for his poetry. I assume that the God of the Waxing Year is not aware that he will have another

inning in another six months. If he were, it would take the edge off the poetic intensity both of his being unrequited and of his being dead.

Magic, love, life and death, and the passage of the seasons are all put together in one poetic hopper, and the brew (*The White Goddess* is full of brew) is the inspiration of the poet. The White Goddess system prevailed three or four thousand years ago, and an opposite system (patrilineal and patriarchal) has prevailed ever since. But, says Mr. Graves, System Number One is the right one for a poet. Under the patriarchal system, we have love, life and death, and the passage of the seasons, but not magic. We have exchanged magic for fathers, which is bad for poetry.

Poetically speaking, therefore, the only people around, both then and now, are the White Goddess and these two up-again, down-again, begin-again gods. What happens if I, a woman, want to write poetry? I have to be the White Goddess. There's no other woman around to be.

Mr. Graves makes this perfectly clear, and clear that it is not easy.

A woman who concerns herself with poetry should, I believe, either be a silent Muse and inspire the poets by her womanly presence . . . or she should be the Muse in a complete sense; she should be in turn Arianrhod, Blodeuwedd and the Old Sow of Maenawr Penardd who eats her farrow, [Welsh aspects of the White Goddess] and should write in each of these capacities with antique authority. She should be the visible moon: impartial, loving, cruel, wise.

The White Goddess is also capricious, in spite of the fact that she seems to operate with clockwork regularity. She is woman in three ages, three seasons, and three different places, which should give her leeway to have a multiplicity of varied characteristics. But she has a distinct and, I think I can fairly say, rather limited personality. To put it succinctly, she is a fiend.

All this works out well and is quite thrilling for the male poet, granted he can look at the visible moon and believe that it is in love with him. I can't, of course, being a woman. I am practicing looking at it and believing that it is I. It is a testimonial to the power of Mr. Graves's theory that I find this easier and almost possible.

Mr. Graves permits the male poet to make some particular woman his Muse or incarnation of the White Goddess as long as the woman doesn't become so domestic and virtuous that she ceases to harry him. If she's too domestic, he won't write poetry. Poetic love is bad, or illicit, love.

This is all right with me, but, as a woman poet, I am not allowed to make any particular man my White God. There is no such God. I might have had Apollo, but Mr. Graves is against him. The Greek philosophers, who were opposed to magical poetry, dethroned the White Goddess and developed rational poetry celebrating Apollo. Apollo is reasonable and true poetry is not. True poetry raises the hairs on the back of the neck.

The reason, he says, "why the hairs stand on end, the skin crawls and a shiver runs down the spine when one writes or reads a true poem is that a true poem is necessarily an invocation of the White Goddess . . . the ancient power of fright and lust—the female spider or the queen-bee whose embrace is death."

All my life I have had to do things like wear shoes, go to dancing school, study arithmetic, be polite, go to cocktail parties, take vitamins, and wash dishes. I would love to have shivers run down my spine. The beautiful phrase, antique authority, excites me. How can I help but be delighted with the idea of being an ancient power of fright and lust? It should be easy. It is supposed to be fatally easy to strip off the trappings of civilization.

It is surprisingly difficult.

I have no trouble with the folds, nor will most women, poets or not. Early in 1957, Mr. Graves lectured on the White Goddess in the United States. I wonder if he realized that, on the occasion I heard him, the uneasy and uncanny giggling in the audience came from women who were in the process of turning themselves into White Goddesses. I don't know about women in matriarchic societies, but both the strength and the weakness of women in patriarchal societies is that they take everything personally. If you do this, you can be as anyfold as you wish.

Women in patriarchal societies are brought up to try to be ladies, whch on the whole means to behave like gentlemen. When such a woman feels it is no longer any go with the God of the Waxing Year, she says, "Go," adding something like "I'm sure you can make some other woman happy." Not the White Goddess. She says, "Drop dead," and the god does. If he doesn't, she gets someone to make him.

Of course, metaphorically speaking, gentlemanly behavior in this case could thoroughly gum up the passage of the seasons. Unmetaphorically speaking, if I, as a woman poet in the twentieth century, said, "Drop dead," and they did, I would soon be in so much trouble that I would have no time to write poetry at all.

But let us assume that to write good poetry I must be illicit and ungentlemanly. Even so, I incline to certain kinds of poetic subject matter and poetry which Mr. Graves won't let me have.

The first is juvenilia. A White Goddess couldn't have juvenilia, and if she did she would throw them away. But as far as I can tell the White Goddess never grew up. She never went through a phase, or an impressionable age, or learned anything, like how to make pot holders or how to distinguish between different kinds of men. She just is. I don't know why, but I have a feeling she isn't very clean.

Unfortunately for me, I grew up. I went through an impressionable period, and there was a patriarchal figure around at the time. I was supposed to learn to distinguish between men. One basis was that some wanted *only one thing* and some wanted several. The patriarchal figure had evidently wanted several, including me, so I got the idea that safety was in numbers.

Being licit and gentlemanly is staid. I understand why Mr. Graves, a patriarchal figure himself, finds patriarchal society boresome. But patriarchal societies offer me, and, I suspect from reading his book, him, a charming compensation—romantic notions. In and of themselves, romantic notions aren't poems, but blow them up, decorate them, send them aloft, and they can be.

The White Goddess is impartial. I take it this means that she likes the God of the Waning Year just as well as the God of the Waxing Year—or just as little. Because of my romantic notions, which are more rock-ribbed and indestructible than my gentlemanliness, I find it almost impossible to be impartial. I like some waxing and waning gods much better than others. Some I could love to utter distraction. This is not White Goddessy. She is destructive. Loving someone to utter distraction is, depending upon what happens, either constructive or self-destructive. Being self-destructive in this way is proper for men poets, but not for women. Clearly it is my father's fault if I feel this way. I do. What I want to know is, why can't it be poetical for me, too?

I am not allowed to love to utter distraction, so I can't be unrequited either. A big dollop of poetic subject matter is ruled out.

Maybe there is a moment between waxing and waning gods when Mr. Graves's attention is distracted, and I could slip being unrequited in.

But I think not. I think this is the moment when I should swoop savagely like a female spider in an impartial sort of way.

I can understand the fascination of the White Goddess. The rest of us being perverse, indifferent people are fascinating. Why shouldn't she be indifferent when she always knows that another god is on the way? All her needs are neatly taken care of. I suspect she is so indifferent that she wouldn't have either the necessary tension or the necessary energy to write poetry at all.

Well, what can I write about? Men poets are supposed to write poems praising the White Goddess. I can write poems praising me. This I like, but I think it might be hard to sustain.

It is particularly hard to sustain when the waxing and waning gods with whom one happens to be acquainted have also grown up in a patriarchal society. One God of the Waxing Year on whom I had my cold blue (White-Goddess-type) eye described to me what he felt would be the perfect relationship with literary women (he liked White Goddesses in the plural). "First," he said, "I'd make love to them (this is a euphemism). Then I'd give them ideas." He has it all wrong. I am supposed to give *him* ideas.

If one is literary, many waxing and waning gods derive their greatest pleasure from pointing out literary lapses: one does not know, for example, how to place the word "only," or has not really mastered the correct rhythms of English.

Here a new element enters: some of the time they know what they are talking about and I learn something. Little boys in patriarchal societies, even democratic ones, know all sorts of things which little girls don't. This starts when your brother knows the makes and years of all the automobiles, and you don't care. As time goes on, men gather exact and detailed knowledge of all sorts of esoterica of which women have barely heard.

If you are a woman, it can be exciting to have them tell you how to connect a sump pump, what parity is, or how to scan sprung rhythm. You go and surreptitiously get out of the library the book they were raving about while you were wondering why their eyebrows grew like that. Somewhere in this not uncommon situation, or in my feelings about it, is some poetic subject matter. Isn't there?

Mr. Graves would say no. The White Goddess has *all* the wisdom and she imparts it to the poet. There's no allowance for a situation in which he tells her a thing or two.

I am so patriarchally degenerate that I even feel there is something I might learn from Mr. Graves. Must he insist that instead I should eat him up?

Aside from my praising me, what have I left in the way of poetic subject matter?

At the very moment the White Goddess theory sprang full-blown from Mr. Graves's head, he had on his desk a little box which he never knew until later was ornamented with a design celebrating the White Goddess of an African tribe. This, he says, might be coincidence, but more likely was an unconscious inspiration.

I had a similar inadvertent experience. I took some notes on Mr. Graves's book, and when I came to read them over, I found something (my handwriting is poor) that read: "The woman poet must write as a worm." Of course I had intended to write woman, but this is no joke. There is something in it, and I must have known it subconsciously. The White Goddess has the capacity to assume different shapes: she becomes a bitch, an otter, a falcon, a black hen, or a sow, in all of which manifestations she pursues men.

This mystic sign convinced me that as a woman poet my next move must be to write a poem about turning myself into a worm. In a trice, I did it. At present I am humping my way along what appears to be a very large highway looking for a man to pursue.

But there is something wrong. I feel queer.

I have just realized what it is. As a worm, I am bisexual. Now I have sat down on the edge of the highway to think this over. Can I pursue myself? Do I want to?

It's going to be an exciting poem and quite unique. Graves is right. I *should* write as the White Goddess. It opens up hitherto unexplored vistas.

I've figured out what to do. I am destructive and I have cut myself in half. I have also figured out who I am going to pursue. I'm not sure yet which one of us is which, but we will both be along, any year now, in hot pursuit. Tallyho, Mr. Graves.

Me as White Goddess

The Fleers of Backford English

ON MY FIRST VISIT TO ROME I KNEW NO Italian, and I immediately needed a dictionary. On a hand-cart in the Via Cavour I found an Italian-English and English-Italian one, compiled by Prof. W. Backford. It was the eighth edition, revised and corrected, so it looked sound.

I didn't expect Italian to be easy. The sun was brilliant; the buildings were a hot orange; automobiles were charging at motor scooters and motor scooters were roaring at each other; in the middle of it all a policeman with white gloves too long in the fingers was conducting an invisible orchestra, and I was told the word for accident is *disgrazia*. The word for confusion or turmoil is *trambusto*, which seemed possible when I looked at what was happening to the traffic. *Imbarazzo*, according to Prof. Backford, is embarrassment, or pinch. That was the way things were the first few days.

Prof. W. Backford sounded as if he might be British. Many of the people who write phrase books and dictionaries for English-speaking travelers are British, which makes it difficult for us, because when we go shopping we have to find out first what camiknickers are before we know if we want them. Though they try to help us out, as in a section called "General Difficulties," which goes like this: "What do you want? I don't know you. I don't want to speak to you. Don't bother me! Go away! That will do. I shall call a policeman.

Help! This man is following me everywhere. That man. I want to see the American Consul."

I didn't expect Italian to be easy, but I didn't expect to have to learn Backford English first before I could begin on Italian. But things often are strange in foreign countries. You have to accept them and try to overbrow them. For this, you need raciness, which, according to Backford, is the English for *forza di spirito*. Any place where force of spirit is raciness is fine with me.

On second thought, I realized that Prof. Backford is not wholly English. I believe he is half English, the offspring of a lord with a racy spirit, who spent a night or so in a Tuscan town, and departed for England unaware that behind him he had left something of the mother country and a future lexicographer.

Backford has never been in England, but he thinks about it often. Backford wonders about the father whom he has never seen and whom he imagines as tall and blond. He deplores his own sparkling brown eyes and smooth tan skin. When he speaks English, the Italian precision of his vowels worries him. Yet when he speaks Italian, he sounds foreign. He looks wistfully after British tourists and haunts English tearooms, where he orders marmalade and crumpets. Though it occurs seldom, because he is poor, his greatest pleasure is to have a meal in a truly British hotel, such as the Brufani Palace in Perugia, where the dining-room voices are subdued to a British quiet, and the menu offers English specialties like *jambon de Yorck*.

Piled up in Backford's small dusty room are many English dictionaries, and he studies them until late at night. He is without snobbery: all English words are equal to him and equally glorious. He does not know that some have gone

out of style. Sometimes when it gets late, and his eyes are tired, his pencil slips. And sometimes as his vision blurs, a word slips off one page, finds elsewhere another word it likes, and joins it. In the morning, Backford happily accepts what he finds, unaware that it has coined itself. These evenings are the center of Backford's life, and its fulfillment: he is making something which may help the British travelers he admires so much.

I had to get a couple of other dictionaries, including a larger Italian-English and English-Italian one, and a Webster's *New International Dictionary*, second edition, unabridged, to find out the meanings of many of Backford's words. Some are words I just didn't happen to know about; for example: to conglobe, to evulgate, to glomerate, to impark, to manducate, to scantle, and to moil. These mean, respectively: to roll up into a ball, to publish, to pile up, to ring with gardens, to eat, to cut up small, and to drudge or overexert yourself (another word for this is overply).

Backford has a secret vice: though London is his Mecca, and he tells himself that it must be grander, infinitely more fulgent and supern, he is in love with Rome. When he goes there, he takes a holiday from crumpets and finds the food extraordinarily saporific. He is leisurely over his refections, and drinks a good deal of wine. Then a delicious dribblet steals over him, in which he forgets that he can never be British. (Dribblet is *inerzia*, and, I believe, means inertia with fountains.) Backford eats in an outdoor café.

There are some Backford words to which the English we know gives no clue. In fact, knowing any English ahead of time uncliuws one (this means undo, doubtless originally in Welsh). To dreal, for instance, means to elongate. To decumb is to put down sprawlingly. Fimsy is thin. A fleer (a cousin once removed of a leer) is a trick or joke, as are also an obreption and a subreption, which seem to be of Scottish origin. The first sounds more obvious (a practical fleer) and the second more underhand.

Backford has a poetic nature: in his English a premature baby is a castling. In his wanderings he has listened to Italian church bells, and when he comes to the word *suonare*, he translates it "clang, knoll, tingle, tink," an onomatopoetic conglobation. He has listened to Italians talking in the streets: he knows that if one of them attles long enough, he may exulcerate the other. They will begin to bisker, and it will all end in a brangle.

As he walks along in a dream of dictionaries, words leap in his head and he notes them down, not always sure where they have come from. To him they sound like English. They must be English. Agrestical, for example, means rustic or wild, or both. Insaurate means restored. A morsure is a bite or a mouthful, perhaps by a person who wears dentures. Oblectation is pleasure, and sorriness (poor Backford!) is poverty.

With some of Backford's words, one feels one knows what they mean, but one is wrong. What is a dorr—one of those faces with a ring in its teeth to knock with? No, a dorr is a bumblebee. I thought gamashes must be the things on Roman ceilings—gold clouds, garlands, angels, shields, naked ladies, *trompe l'œil* columns. No, gamashes are something very British. They are gaiters.

Backford likes the Roman ceilings and he knows that whatever is on them scambles and scruffles, two words which mean the same thing. Backford hopes they will never disgarnish the ceilings of Rome.

Where did Backford find the verb to jety? His synonym

151

is to flirt, but I think he is trying to be discreet and British, for obviously it means to make love (*amoreggiare*). When Backford went to the Piazza del Campidoglio, I wonder if he looked up at the second floor of the Capitoline Museum. If he did and the window was open, he saw Cupid and Psyche in marble, jetying with their naked backs to the window. I am sure that he reflected on the fact that Roma is *amor* backwards, just like Cupid and Psyche.

Backford has his moments of genius: he offers the tourists many words at once more economical and richer than their own. Untreacable means impossible to find again once you've lost it, and inenarrable means impossible to speak of. Elutriate (from elute, to rinse) means to pour water carefully. For years, we have needed the word incrassate, which means to get fat and/or rich. And rapts—a combination word meaning abduction and religious ecstasy. If you are in a rapts, you wish to be abducted supernly, that is, celestially.

In spite of his objections, Backford's publishers forced him to keep his dictionary small. But he has squeezed into it some splendid words that cannot be found elsewhere. For instance, to darindle. This means to shall, but obviously it means to shall in a particular way, perhaps more Roman than British. Backford darindles through Rome, not shalling so hard that he wears himself out, not moiling or overplying, but just shalling casually along, stopping on the way for a morsure of ice cream or an espresso in the Piazza Navona. If he doesn't like it when he has darindled to where he is going, he can always divindle back.

Backford is perhaps at his most inspired when he takes an English word and gives it a new meaning. To pill is to despoil. To jade is to give in. He is also clever at making verbs out of nouns: to fuzz is to weaken the fibers of, and to nick is to encounter someone at the right moment.

Only very occasionally does Backford admit himself defeated by a word. One example is the verb to cere, for which the Italian is *passare la cera*. This seems to mean to pass the beeswax. Backford gives no further information. So I have decided that to cere is a conglobation which means to carry a torch while not being able to hold a candle to, a condition in which one feels very lown (*buono a nulla*).

All the time I was studying Backford English, I sensed that in its creation was hidden a definite, though unexpressed, purpose. Backford English was meant for something, but what?

At first I thought it might be for writing Italian guidebooks in English. The Italians are very accommodating about providing such guidebooks, and their English is specially designed for this purpose. "Gorgeous and picturesque points of view, clear and distant backgrounds rise everywhere from the soil in an uninterrupted waving. The ravaged spleen of bygone times, mixed up with the present splendour, shines as a serene vision from the heights of Eternity." This is Rome, where "numerous styles, ages, and memories are superposed in very little room. . . . That makes of Rome a Paradise for archaeologists and learned people, but these people don't detain the secret of her beauty and grandeur." (The author thinks it takes an artist.)

Still, there are many words in Backford that I have never found in the guidebooks. The guidebooks sometimes obtund things, and once you master him, Backford is always lucent. After giving this some thought, I realized what Backford had in mind.

Going to Rome is frustrating for a penner like me. Everything you can say about Rome has already been written by someone. You can have it according to Henry Adams, or Nathaniel Hawthorne, or Mark Twain, or many other talented penners. By 1869 Mark Twain was already frustrated. All he could find to do was to write a whole chapter about the history of the Colosseum, without—this was a point of pride—once using the phrase "butchered to make a Roman holiday." Backford would have approved: he also dislikes clichés. He might have offered Mark Twain "scantled to make a Roman vacancy."

Yet, all the time, you know that it's you who has discovered Rome. I mean, it is I. So Backford English is for me to describe Rome as it has never been described before. Because I do detain the secret of its beauty and grandeur. I imbosom it. In fact, I cere it.

Rome is eternally darindling, and who knows where? It is full of curiosities: in this lucent city, there is a lighthouse without anything to light. A church in the shape of a dorr uprises in a tower twisted together at the top like a paper bag. There is the Colosseum, which someone said looked like an abandoned dorrhive, though actually, pilled as it is, it looks like something abnormously natural, the craters of the moon—a full moon in an unobnubilate sky, seen on a noctambulation. Something abnormously unnatural is the house in the Via Gregoriana, whose door is trying to take a great morsure, perhaps of an obelisk. There is one in the next square, and there are many others, fimsy and drealed against the sky, scattered around the city.

The fountains of Rome darindle most of all, elancing sea monsters, naiads, tritons, Neptunes, and Moors, and jets of water that all the raffs and cits of Rome dibble their hands in. Everything that can be is eluted and bedashed.

In a garden in the Palazzo del Conservatori, a crouched, skew little man elutriates water out of a wine sack. A Triton perflates it through a horn. There are dolphins everywhere in pairs, raddling their tails together. All over Rome, water clangs, knolls, tingles, and tinks, even in the church below the Church of San Clemente where it runs in fuscous caverns, while above, in the mosaic of the apse, the faithful, as lambs, imbrue their feet. Not to mention that decumbed glomeration, the Trevi Fountain. I could overslaugh with oblectation when I think of it.

History is apeak in this city. Everything is up and down and glomerated in layers. How many generations have incrassated here! How many have lived in sorriness! All now are inhumate. How frangible the monuments, yet how astunding their curious durity! Much is excrescent, much decrescent, and all of it is on display, even Saint Teresa in her rapts, watched by marble men in theater boxes. But, insolate under the austral sun, bedaggled, bedusted, and fuliginous, these tarmished ruins still are fulgent.

Before such sights, the senses actuate, while the mind fuzzes. Overswayed and lown, you feel you might jade to morbose and nocent thoughts. Pretermit them. Where history is so decumbed, it is natural to feel mistimed. Offward the farmost outstreets lead from the agrestical Campagna into Rome, and all roads will always continue to darindle there. Oh supern, fulvous city, insaurate and uninsaurate, pilled yet imparked, incompressible, inenarrable, full of raciness!

Shortly before I left Rome I saw a sign scrawled in chalk on the wall of the Palazzo Barberini, which said, like this: MUSA. I was overswayed by oblection to find that someone was invoking the Muse.

If I hadn't studied Backford, I might have had my feelings hurt. I might have brooded about those two upside-down V's, which, they tell me, mean the opposite of Viva, that is, "Down with." I might have thought USA meant me. But studying Backford English gives you a new point of view. It oversets things.

Before I departed, I went back to look for MUSA again, but it was untreacable. It had nicked me.

IV

Jumping at the World

How to Avoid Emotional Maturity

OPENING A NEWSPAPER OR MAGAZINE these days is like opening Pandora's box. The moment you do, someone swarms all over you and asks a series of personal questions.

Are you lovable? Tactful? Optimistic? Irritable? Disgruntled? Sorry for yourself? Do you keep up? How observing are you? Are you well-rounded?

Some people feel compelled to answer all the questions asked them, and others, more blessed, don't. I am one of those who have to. How do you fight a cold? they ask. I put down the magazine and tell them. Splitting nails? No, but on my left little finger— In a radio speech during the 1956 election campaign, Adlai Stevenson asked, "Have the last four years been good for you?" "Yes and no, Adlai," I began eagerly, and I went on to tell him all about them, missing the rest of his speech.

This is an addiction. I realized I had it badly when, on a rainy day in a summer house, I took an intricate test which both a husband and wife were supposed to answer in opposing columns. I am neither, but I pretended to be both. We were incompatible.

Unlike Adlai, who sounded interested, most of the question askers are determined to prove to me that I am not whatever-it-is, so that they can tell me to reexamine and

159

reshape myself. They succeed. I think I am well-rounded here and there, but I feel I had better make sure. I always turn out to be square.

Their tone is bland, but their technique is stealthy.

There is always one right answer. Considering how inadequate I am, it is surprising that I can recognize it. Here is an example from a test to gauge one's independence. You are supposed to check one of the three statements, as being most like yourself.

A. Time often hangs heavy on my hands, especially if some certain person is away or unavailable.

B. My own duties and responsibilities, along with what I do for others, keep me busy and content.

C. Bored? Not unless I'm flat on my back. As long as I can kick up my heels and go, time flies.

A, who is in love, is overdependent. As you will see later, this is what "in love" means. C is irresponsible. B is the head of the class, though I can think of almost no one who could honestly check it aside from Beth in *Little Women*, who wasn't a bit independent.

Here is another series from the same test.

A. I'm not apt to think much about convention and dignity. I sort of follow the crowd in matters of propriety.

C. There are no rules that can't be broken if a matter were sufficiently challenging—especially silly customs.

B. My world is built on substantiality and convention, and I believe in living in it in a dignified, respectable manner.

Note how they try to trick me. Just in case I am getting into a habit and expect to find the right answer in the middle, they have stuck good old B down at the bottom. A is still the hat-over-the-windmill character of the previous group, and C is the moony one.

I have checked A in the first group and C in the second, and I am getting good and mad. I'd like to point out that I am quite busy a lot of the time. Has anyone said I didn't get my work done? Well, then. Why can't I just once in a while, wander around thinking about some certain person? And how could my world be built on substantiality and convention? My world is, of course, built on me.

When I finished the test, they told me I was "the personification of human variableness." This isn't true. While that smug B is all over the place being busy, dignified, and good, who is faithfully thinking about some certain person?

Often they arrange the test in such a way that, after I have taken it in a humble and cooperative spirit, they turn on me. Is your mother-in-law an asset? they asked me. I don't have a mother-in-law, but I obligingly made one up, based on someone I thought could be she, and took the test. She wasn't too bad, but she wasn't a terrific asset either.

When I got to the end of the test, and totted it up, they told me sternly that I should think seriously about my own behavior and ask myself if I were a good daughter-in-law. This is backhanded. They asked me a straight question about my mother-in-law, not about me.

It is my fault for answering the questions. But how does one acquire an addiction? One way is by constantly being offered the opportunity to indulge it.

Never in the whole history of human endeavor have so many people been so busily engaged in pointing out to so many other people what was wrong with them, and how they could improve themselves. It makes me wonder. If there are many who get as low marks on these tests as I do, the country is in a bad way.

Owing to my addiction, I have discovered that most of my basic ideas are, if not off, a little awry.

An example was a test called "How Lovable Are You?" I thought I knew what lovable meant, but I began to doubt that I did when they asked, "Are you honest and aboveboard about money, sex, religion, etc.?" I certainly didn't know what they meant by etc., but I knew about honest and aboveboard. I gathered they wanted to know, for some obscure reason of their own, if I spoke my mind about money, sex, and religion. Frequently I don't, so I got a bad mark. I kept expecting them to ask me if I were affectionate, but they didn't. They asked if I were sloppy and carelessly groomed at home, and I got another black mark.

It was the same with "Are You Impulsive?" Impulsive means to act on impulse, and an impulse is a sudden incitement to action. I didn't think being impulsive was a cure-all for everything, but I thought it might be useful occasionally. On the whole I thought it an attractive quality.

I couldn't have been more wrong. In this test, I came out middling. "You can greatly reduce your mistakes and regrets if you apply better judgment and control," they told me. The straight A person in this test is told, "You wisely and maturely curb your emotions when you feel an urge to act impulsively."

I do no better when we come to the important questions of love, marriage, mates, etc., and I think you know what I mean by etc. In this field, my life always needs reshaping.

"Are people in love usually happy?" a column in the *Daily Mirror* asked me. "Yes," I said promptly, thinking they meant two people who were in love with each other. They did mean two people who were in love with each other, but I was still wrong.

"People 'in love' are very much like people who have manic-depressive insanity—they have periods of exalted ecstasy and of profound depression. . . . Each one's happiness or unhappiness depends almost entirely on the other's attitudes, words, tones of voice, etc. *People who allow their lives to depend on someone else* [their italics] can never be continuously happy."

They didn't say "continuously" before.

The *Daily Mirror* is not the only publication that thinks "in love" is queer. Elsewhere it is referred to as "love neurosis." You should get it tamped down or over with before making the important decision to marry.

The *Daily Mirror* was anxious for me to get things straight: they said that Public Affairs Pamphlet No. 161, *So You Think It's Love!* would be a big help to me in this situation.

The idea of love being public affairs convinced me that I had had the wrong idea all along. So I, deluded A-C, personification of human variableness, sent for it.

It turned out to be addressed to teen-agers. Apparently everyone over this age has solved this problem. I am not only variable, unlovable, and middling impulsive, I am backward.

However, Public Affairs Pamphlet No. 161 is revolutionary. It says people do not fall in love at all. This is a false notion which "goes back to the days when people were apt to say 'love is blind.' "

People grow into love. You cannot love someone until you know him very well. And you cannot do it at all until you become the right kind of person, at which point you will attract the right kind of person, who is dependable, even-tempered, thoughtful, kind, considerate, helpful, friendly, honest, and affectionate.

The writer of the pamphlet says that young people "have almost come to think of these qualities as old-fashioned." But, he says happily, "people are old-fashioned. The same kind of people have been coming into the world with the same needs and the same drives for thousands of years."

I agree with this, but I had thought that for thousands of years the same kind of people had been falling in love. I got this idea from some old-fashioned people like Catullus and Shakespeare. Now I am quite mixed up about what has been going on and what is old-fashioned. A boy scout, for instance, certainly isn't old-fashioned. A boy scout is trustworthy, loyal, helpful, friendly, courteous, kind, obedient, cheerful, thrifty, brave, clean, and reverent. Is it old-fashioned, new-fashioned, or just plain inept of me that I have never attracted a boy scout or considered one as a possible mate?

I was brought up on *Little Women*, and I have as much desire to become the right kind of person as the next one. In an article in the *Ladies Home Journal*, I found a definitive list of the qualifications for a good wife, or what they call her basic personality factors. The list is too long to give all of here, but among other things, she is agreeable, responsible, thrifty, conservative, well-integrated, free from tension, foresighted, discreet, alert, basically religious, optimistic, and confident.

She is not a crusader or a reformer. She chooses friends who are honest, conservative, and who conform to accepted standards of behavior.

She dislikes carelessness in dress and habitual tardiness.

She likes people older than herself, which will help her to be a good daughter-in-law.

She believes in doing right for its own sake. She seems to know exactly what it is: the *Journal* says she has always tried to do right and has no worries.

As far as sex is concerned (this entry is under the heading "Realism"), she accepts her role as her husband's partner.

After I had read the article, the good wife haunted me. I felt I had known her somewhere, and after some thought it came back to me. I went to school with her, and we called her "Teacher's Pet."

The *Journal* didn't want to discourage me too much. They kindly remarked that a poor showing compared with this ideal shouldn't make me "give up hope of a happy marriage." But, deficient as I am in these basic qualifications, I must be thoughtful and deliberate in choosing a husband. I must work hard all the time to develop compensating virtues.

Even with a prefrontal lobotomy, I couldn't make it. I can't, and in school didn't, even classify to be a friend of the good wife. If I hadn't been trying so hard to keep up with what the press of America wants me to be, I wouldn't care. I didn't like her in school, and I don't think I would now. Anyway, she's older than I am. She sounds older than God.

From the *Journal*, and various other sources, one learns that a good husband must be as many things as a good wife. He must drink sparingly, get up without prodding, get to work on time, handle personal spending well, avoid taking chances, and a great deal more.

Everyone wants to help you if you are wondering whether someone will make a suitable mate. From a psychologist I heard on the radio I learned that there was no way of selecting a suitable mate, but that there was a way of rejecting an unsuitable one. She gave a list of twenty qualities, some of which he shouldn't have and some of which he should. Ever since I have been checking everyone off, and it is amazing how easy it is to rule them all out. Soon I am going to be entirely without any unsuitable possible mates, which seems a pity, but it can't be helped.

But I am getting discouraged. It dawns on me that from this school I will never be able to graduate.

Everyone is getting altogether too demanding and choosy. The most completely exclusive example I have found of this attitude is in *The Art of Loving,* by Erich Fromm. Dr. Fromm says there is almost no love around because only a person who is totally concentrated and dedicated, who is always disciplined and never trivial, who treats love as a fine art and devotes a lifetime to it, has the capacity to love, or can be said to love. Such people are very rare, but if one does not love, sex and marriage are dust and ashes and not a good idea.

This puts us all in a difficult position. Suppose that I am going along, trying to be mature and aware, and I am aware enough to know that I am about halfway to disciplined maturity. Someone stops me, and I feel a whiff of love, which of course is really that old second-rate "in love." Am I to say, "No, no, go away. Wait until I am finished, browned, done to a turn and ready to serve. Until then, you and I are not real"?

This position is so intrinsically difficult that I think there is something wrong with it. For one thing, it is snobbish.

Only a very superior person can be said to love. None but the emotionally mature deserve the fair.

I refuse to believe that love is only for the favored few. I agree with Mr. E. M. Forster, who says it is a republic. Nor is love to be defined by how well it works: does a clock lose its name if it strikes thirteen?

Everyone would like to have a whole loaf of the highest quality, but if he does not acquire one, is it necessary to say that he has no capacity to taste bread?

The ultimate aim of all these writers is to make me and everyone else emotionally mature. I have made a bold decision: I have decided not to be. If I do it their way, I have to accept the fact that there can be no satisfactions in life until I have reached emotional maturity. If I don't, I can imagine that I am enjoying myself as I go along.

I am not against emotional maturity. I think the emotionally mature person is quite all right in its place. It's a nice quiet place to visit, but I wouldn't want to live there. I wouldn't call it living.

So I have done some of what these writers call analytical research on the subject. I have studied all the descriptions I can find of the emotionally mature person in order to be able to avoid it. Here are my findings for anyone else who may feel the same way:

In general, the emotionally mature person gives everyone as little trouble as possible. It (as we go along, you will understand why I have a tendency to call it it) is always ready to make suggestions, to participate and to cooperate, but even when it knows it is right, it never tries to impose its ideas on others.

It has no trouble making decisions, but it never makes

them impetuously or quickly. This somehow guarantees that it is always pleased with the results.

It is moderate in everything, and so never feels guilty. Guilt is so emotionally immature that even if you have a reason for feeling guilty, you are not supposed to.

It always takes a positive attitude toward life, and never, no matter how much life is jumping around, yelling, and cursing, allows itself to feel that life is too much for it. It treats life like a nice, but temporarily naughty, child.

It keeps on an even keel emotionally. It does not become despondent, and never cries, not even *lacrimae rerum*. On the other hand, it does not get joyous or euphoric, because that would be manic of it, and not emotionally mature.

It always plans for the future. You mustn't call it up and suggest it do something on the spur of the moment.

It has a sense of humor—but wait. A sense of humor is not what you think it is. It is the capacity to laugh at one-self, but not at others.

It does things for others, but never in order to be appreciated. If it feels that it might be wanting to be appreciated, it would have to stop doing things for others.

It believes it will achieve success by cooperation, not individual effort.

There are no single people who are emotionally mature. But the emotionally mature person is very slow to fall into anyone's arms, and very particular about its mate. Once mated, it promptly accepts its mate as it is, but is understanding. It constantly asks itself if it is doing the right thing and saying the right thing at the right moment, and it never discusses problems with its husband when he is tired. If it is a husband, it expresses interest in its wife's housework. It is essential that both husband and wife be emotionally mature. Everyone is tiptoeing around being so considerate that, if one of them is not, he or she is likely to feel like a mental case.

The emotionally mature person knows sex is a good thing, but difficult, so it is patient about it. If it finds sex isn't going well, it gets more information, not from a little more sex, but from a marriage counselor or a book. The Public Affairs people can recommend it a book called *Building Sex into Your Life*, from which it can learn to build it in, hammer it down, and fasten it with a toggle bolt.

In fact, it always seeks advice from proper authorities. It never does anything bad, so it has very little experience to draw on. It has to consult authorities. I think there must be quite a lot of emotionally mature people around already, because there certainly are a lot of authorities.

It has a group activity and a hobby. It is not afraid of anything. It does not need anyone. It can eat everything.

A human being is perverse, passionate, and unexpected, impulsive, excitable, and full of dreams, hilarious and dolorous, irritating and inspired, dedicated and trivial, and gets into a lot of trouble. I am going out to get a breath of air, to strike thirteen, and to see if there are any human beings still around.

On Being a Little Bit Sick

MY PRESENT THESIS IS SERIOUS: nowadays there is something wrong with the way people are a little bit sick.

Let me recall to you how we grew up. Aside from contagious diseases, we had a bad cold (or a sniffle), bronchitis, the grippe, or a stomach upset. If we had a temperature, we went to bed. We stayed there, drinking orange juice and a lot of water, and taking aspirin, until our temperature had been normal for a day. Then we got up and went back to school, feeling wobbly and interesting. Each of these things took a certain length of time. I always had a cold for five days, bronchitis for about ten, the grippe for a week, and a stomach upset for three or four days. A stomach upset was caused by something I ate, not by something that was going around.

Ah, the serene, secure, peaceful world of our childhood! I remember dear Granny, who always used to prune the maple trees, stoke the furnace, play the *Rhapsody in Blue*, and fill the croup kettle herself, because no one else could ever do it right, laying her hand on my forehead and saying, "Feverish." In a trice, I would be in bed, cutting out paper dolls and having meals on a tray. I remember that unmistakable, deliciously excruciating soreness in the throat, which was not tonsillitis because, unlike the pampered youngsters of today, I had no tonsils, but which meant, in any case, that everyone was going to have to pay attention to me for a while. Oh, the homely words, "You ought to be in bed." Ah, the ecstatic pleasure, just as the lilacs began to bud in the spring, of gagging on a tablespoonful of dark-brown, thick, gluey Keppler's Malt and Iron Iodide. And one of my happiest and most nostalgic memories is myself at the age of twelve, propped up in bed on two pillows, sick as a pig, devouring *Ghosts* by Ibsen, and trying to figure out what everyone in the play was being so dire about.

Nowadays I'd know. I'd know the symptoms. I'd manage to have several of them.

What do we have now? Viruses. Viruses can be anything from a sore throat to a headache to strange aches in places you didn't have them with the grippe. Viruses can give you a temperature of 103° one day and nothing the next, during which you do not feel very bad, or they can give you just 99° for a month on end, during which you feel fierce.

The medical profession is no help whatever. As everyone knows, they have lost the bedside manner of the old family doctor. In fact, there's almost no bedside. Today's doctors hate to leave their nice machines. They don't suggest your going to bed because they don't want you to get in the habit of enjoying being sick there. So everyone stays up when they're sick and children wander around in their pajamas.

"A little virus," the doctor tosses off casually, or "low-grade infection." "Low-grade infection" is not reassuring. It sounds lurking and insidious, as if it would eat away at me and soften me up for something worse, and as a matter of fact it will.

If the doctor is somewhat modern, he gives you a wonder drug, after saying airily, "You can take antivirounoduotrethrycin, can't you?" You think so, but, as you leave the office, you begin to wonder. What, you ask yourself, are its fearful aftereffects? What is that curious numbness in the left side of the big toe? Will the toe drop off?

If the doctor is very modern, he doesn't give you anything at all. He says, "Take aspirin every four hours. This has to run its course." Nothing about how long the course is. It's just a virus and you're supposed to wear it out.

Feeling as one does at this time, one needs security, like, for instance, having the grippe. Then one would know what to do and what to tell people. I have tried and tried to suggest to my doctor that I have the grippe or bronchitis, but, if I can get him pried loose from "virus," all he will allow is "respiratory infection."

Even the blissful security of running a temperature is no more. In the old days, anything over normal was a temperature: you were sick. Today, what with competition and overcrowding, you have to run a respectable temperature before you can get any consideration. "Not really a temperature," they say to 99.6°. Many a time, calling on the last reserves of my dwindling strength, I have worked and worked to get my temperature up to 100°, so I could have crust enough to telephone the doctor.

Hence one of the most agonizing dilemmas of modern life, which I am tentatively calling the departure syndrome. You have a scratchy throat, a temperature of 99.4° (almost 6), you feel woozy in the head, and you want to lie down on the sofa in the middle of doing something.

This is the moment when either you are about to go away for a particularly pleasant weekend which cannot be duplicated for a year, or you are summoned to the funeral of a very dear friend or relative.

Of course, you *can* go. If you had to go and cover the finding of the Snark for *Life*, or attend your daughter's wedding, or even get married yourself, you could do it. The hell of this situation is that you don't *have* to. *If you are sick.*

I advise you to lie. Say you have 100.6°. You don't feel well enough to go anyway.

But the trouble with you and me and most of us is that you are a sterling character. You don't lie. You bore yourself and your friends with the following labyrinthine monologue: 99.4° isn't really a temperature. I've often traipsed around the city with a cold and been none the worse. Am I coddling myself? Will everyone think I am a hypochondriac? I do have that peculiar ache in the upper part of my left hip. Is it in my head? Maybe I should take my temperature again. Maybe if I went, it would distract my mind, and I would feel better. And so on.

I can also tell you what will happen. If you go, you will not only feel terrible, but you will have to continue the above conversation with everyone, in hopes that someone will tell you to go to bed. If you don't go, your temperature will immediately go down to 98.4 1/2°. You will feel much worse, because you will know you are a slob, and you will not feel better until you have forced your temperature up again.

This is no way to live.

The difficulty is that I and I suspect, you, don't really believe viruses exist. I never had them when I was a child. Why should I be having them now? Nobody's told me to go to bed. Obviously I can't really be sick. Is this in my head? Maybe—(see above)

But I feel awful.

I feel just awful enough to be a prey to every possible suggestion as to what might be wrong with me. The doctor hasn't told me anything positive (like the grippe), so I turn (1) to the media of public information and (2) to my friends. When one is sick, what else does one have to occupy oneself with?

The media of public information tell me about things like blood-iron weakness, the very mention of which makes me conscious of a slow subterranean seeping out of my arteries of vital iron. I'm not sure where it's seeping. Through the bottoms of my feet? They tell me about the seven danger signals of cancer, at least five of which I have regularly. On one occasion, when I wasn't feeling well at all, I was frightened to death by the report of President Eisenhower's health examination. "There is a good pulse in each foot," it said. I went all over my feet carefully inch by inch, and I didn't have any pulse in either of them. What did it mean?

Friends are worse because their information is more esoteric and definite. "Can you manage without the aspirin?" asks one, tenderly concerned for my welfare. "It destroys the vitamin C in your body." This is the same friend who tells me it's bad for me to have an eggnog, which is all I have strength to concoct. The reason is—let me try to get it straight—that there is something in egg white called avidin, which, uncooked, does something to something in me called biotin, and the result is dry peeling skin, extreme fatigue, muscular pain, nausea and distress around the heart, and mental depression verging on panic. Now how do I feel?

This friend is nowhere near so invidious as the one who knows that it is in my head. This one pauses pregnantly after my heart-rending description of my symptoms, and then, ostensibly offhand, actually avid, asks, "Why do you suppose you got sick right now?" Here the trap door drops out from under me and my tenuous virus.

There are a lot of people around nowadays who have read a little book, or seen a little psychiatrist. They have learned that no one ever catches anything. She does it to herself, for repressed, nefarious reasons, which she had better get right out into the broad light of day. And here is old So-and-So just itching to help her elaborate the seamiest possible interpretation of her activity immediately prior to said temperature.

You cannot get out of it by saying you are run-down. Why are you run-down? You were tired. Why were you tired? You had been overdoing. Why did you feel it necessary to overdo? What were you running away from? What were you trying to conceal from yourself?

With only a little practice, a normally imaginative person can concoct a rich explanation immediately. Just before hitting 99.6°, I had a date with X. X drums his fingers on the table in a way that reminds me of how my mother played the piano. When I was seven, my mother spanked me for breaking the springs in the chaise longue. Note the relationship between my jumping on the springs, X drumming on the table, and my mother tickling the ivories (Tickling? Hmmm, how did that get in here and why?). Note: springs—strings—syringe (Stop it!). I really wanted to break the strings in my mother's piano, because she sprayed my nose when I had a cold. (Why did I have a cold? Hold—cold?—everything. One at a time!) The strings of a violin are made of catgut, and, as it happened, I played the violin. Though I am misinformed (I just looked it up), catgut to me means vocal cords. Hence (are you with me?) I was masking a desire to cut my mother's throat. (It's funny, but I can distinctly remember not masking this desire.)

Anyway, I am guilty about it. One is always guilty. This is why I have a sore throat now.

You can see how easy this is. Try doing it when you do not feel well. Will it bring up your repressed aggressions and clear your nasal passages? No, it will make you feel worse. Because you have just thought of one or two even murkier things which you do not choose to tell old So-and-So right now. Already your busy little mind is working on them. Keep it up and you will discover that not only are you working hard, but you deserve, to get cancer, a heart attack, a brain tumor, etc. Once you realize this, trying to stop thinking about it is like being told not to put beans up your nose.

Please don't think that I am not prepared to take responsibility. It is just that I do not like my responsibility to act like the picture of the baking-powder can on the picture of of the baking-powder can, and so on.

Besides, to be polite, I have to listen to old So-and-So's symptoms, and I do not feel up to it.

The only people who can do anything about the present situation are the doctors. It will be clear to them by now that I don't know anything at all. They had better stop thinking I do. On the other hand, there is no use in their being secretive. I have a library card and can scare myself good and proper if I want to.

In exchange for sharing this valuable bit of information with them, I am prepared to tell them something I *do* know, which they don't. There are two types of people who are a

177

little bit sick, and only two. The first group is those who *know* they have cancer, heart disease, or a brain tumor, and are very, very brave about it all. The second is those who have a stomach upset and know that they are about to die.

I don't wish to be specifically invidious, so I will simply say that many women fall into the first category and many men into the second. The first group is quieter, more easily discouraged, and gets well slowly. These people need a number of friends (preferably without bias) to recite their symptoms to, because they will not be reassured by one friend. People in the second group are noisier, cannot be fobbed off as easily, and recover quickly. They need one person giving them her full attention with hot-water bottles, ice water and tender loving care, which they will snarl at because she cannot imagine how awful they feel, until they suddenly recover, and forget the whole thing.

An eminent authority has divided us all into aggressive and regressive types, depending on what ailments we get under stress, so I will be authoritative too, and call these two groups the compulsive and the repulsive.

Both compulsives and the people who look after repulsives need the doctors to provide something more formalized. If the medical profession has permanently given up the grippe, and other pleasant ailments, the least they can do is provide a mystique or ritual for the present chaotic situation. This should start with at least five minutes of sympathizing with the patient for feeling so bad. A definite prescription should follow. It doesn't have to be like the old one, but it must be definite. Something like: Stay in bed for three days. Get up every hour on the hour and drink one glass of water. After draining it, recite "Invictus" by

On Being a Little Bit Sick

W. E. Henley, taking a deep breath and exhaling hard after each line. Under no circumstances, eat any smoked oysters. On the fourth day, you will feel better. This will give everyone something to do and will take his or her mind off how he or she feels.

As it happens, I am susceptible to low-grade virus infections, and I am on my way to a severe case of subacute, subclinical, symptomatic, infinitesimal microcosm. My friends tell me it can be permanently disabling. I am too sick to go on wearing out viruses for the doctors. If they don't think up something for me to do soon, they will lose me.

Do you know where I will be? I will be in bed, with aches in my bones and a fever, drinking orange juice, reading *The Week-end Book of Ghost Stories* (I have gone downhill, too), and taking it very easy. I will be having the comfortable, reassuring, debilitating grippe, and I shall not get up for seven whole days.

Grippe, anyone?

How I Lost One-and-a-Half
Pounds in Six Weeks

BUT A SHORT TIME AGO I HAD THAT squeezed, bloated feeling that life was passing me by. I weighed a hundred and twenty-seven pounds. Life couldn't help seeing me—I was that solid. But it didn't have to stick around, and it sure wasn't. I mean, life was the one thing that wasn't sticking to my ribs. How could it when so much was sticking there already!

Each time no one said to me, "My, you're thin!" I felt rejected. Sometimes no one said anything at all. I would go home and eat some more barbecued pine nuts. Do you know how many calories there are in one barbecued pine nut? A plenty. Barbecued pine nuts were my only real pleasure. How could I bear to live without them?

The editors of the *Females' Lovely-Home Friend* have asked me to write my dieting experiences to show the other kids that it can be done. This makes me awfully happy because it was the *Friend* that made me realize that I just must lose weight. I had to be blasted out of my bad habits. I had to stop fooling myself that I looked womanly, fulfilled, and lush, when I really looked as if I had been brought up on corn-meal mush. *Which* I was.

I guess I had to read the *Friend* to realize what a fright I was, and how much I hated myself for having put off all those years getting down to business, coming up to scratch, pulling up my socks, buttoning up my lip, biting the bullet, and shaking the lead out of my shoes. How the scales plummeted when I got rid of that lead!

The *Friend* spurred me on as no one else could have by never letting the subject alone, one way or t'other. Every month they showed me wonderful colored pictures of the most yummy-looking things to eat, such as a cheese, whipped cream, and gravy pie, topped with grated almonds, and sizzling with chicken fat. Of course I had to concoct it, and of course I tasted as I went along (those seasonings are *tricky*), and of course I promptly put on five pounds. Then I would turn the sticky page, and find "Once I was Five-Ton Fatima," the story of someone who had just lost eighty pounds on a diet of ground pollen and powdered lichen, stirred together with a little high-protein curd. Never once did the *Friend* stop confronting me with the two horns of my dilemma.

My experiences are sort of different from those of most of the people who have written for the *Friend*. All of them had a horrid time, because people called them names like Fatso, Tubby, Chubby, Blubber, or Mrs. Five-by-Five. It's funny, but nobody ever said to me, "Where do you buy your tents?" or "Look out, you'll break the sidewalk." Mostly it was I who said things. We'd be walking along, and pass an enormous woman, and I'd say, "Am I as fat as that?" and my friend would say "Hmmm," and I'd say, "What do you mean?" and my friend would say, "This is boring." But I knew, though I wouldn't admit it.

As soon as the other people who write to the *Friend* lose fifty pounds, they are buddies with the people who've made nasty remarks. They report that it's fun to be included in

181

their activities. I don't understand why they ever speak to them again, but I guess this shows that once you get rid of that excess poundage, you are a totally new personality.

There's another mysterious thing. A lot of the dieters report that when they were at their fattest, miserably unattractive, hating themselves, and not having fun, along came a sweet considerate person, with a few personal problems of his own, who married them. Then they dieted.

The editors of the *Friend* always want to know if something special started you dieting. Now don't laugh, but with me it was a picture in a magazine, which certainly proves the power of advertising. The picture showed the thinnest girl you've ever seen, standing in a forest, balancing herself with one arm around a tree truck, and with the other flung up in the air in a summons. All she had on was a bra and girdle. I don't remember what they looked like, though I know I was supposed to, but that picture galvanized me. I said to myself, "*That's* what I want to look like." I, too, wanted to be so thin I could stand in a damp forest with practically nothing on and have the confidence to summon —Nature Boy?

Somehow I knew it was now or never, that I'd said "I'm going to diet" for the millionth time for the last time. I pinned that picture right up by the refrigerator, so I'd see it every time I was tempted. And was I tempted!—to take the picture down.

Because after it had been there for a while, all I could think of when I looked at it was, "Why don't you put on some stockings? Your garters are dangling."

I spent the first week talking back to the picture and at the end of it I weighed a hundred and twenty-seven pounds. I had to take more drastic measures.

I knew, because I had read the *Friend* carefully, that it was awfully important to keep a chart of my weight to check my progress. Everyone says that with every few pounds you lose, your popularity increases. I wanted to be sure of exactly what I had lost, so I wouldn't mistake any signs of increasing popularity for something else, like, for instance, lust.

My scales are old-fashioned. You stand on a little platform above a large dial. I've kept them because, unlike the new ones, the dial can be read without your glasses on. My glasses weigh an eighth of a pound.

I knew I had to face up to the *weight* of the evidence! I stood on those scales before breakfast with no clothes on, which is as thin as you can be. I weighed a hundred and twenty-seven. After breakfast, I began to wonder. Had I eaten too much breakfast? I went and weighed myself again, now, of course, with my clothes on. Horrors, I weighed a hundred and thirty and a half. Could my clothes and breakfast weigh three and a half pounds? I took my clothes off and weighed them. They weighed two and three-quarter pounds. I weighed myself again. I was a hundred and twenty-eight.

I was so dismayed that I gasped. In so doing, I held my breath, pulled in my stomach, and tipped back on my heels. I weighed a hundred and twenty-six and a half.

This is how I achieved my first blessed weight loss, and what an encouragement it was to continue! I continued weighing myself five or six times a day.

That was the second week.

It isn't how much you weigh, but how it is distributed. Your hips are supposed to be a little larger than your bust, and your waist ten inches smaller. Measurements are very important: if you ignore them, you will not have a before for your after.

When you take your measurements you must BE HONEST. This means, don't pull the tape measure tight. It's terribly hard not to. Your natural tendency is to line the tape measure up, preferably on a round number. Movie stars' measurements are always in round numbers. Nobody who is glamorous is in eighths and sixteenths.

Alas, I was 35 1/8, 26 7/16, and 36 7/8. I had to chop off those nasty fractions. And I had to watch it closely so I wouldn't go over the edge into another fraction.

If you use a cloth tape measure, under no circumstances wash it. It will shrink and increase your measurements by as much as half an inch. The metal kind is more reliable, except that it is difficult to get curved around you, and, when you do, cold.

I spent most of the third week measuring myself, because each time it came out a little different. If I did it honestly, with the tape measure loose, it fell off. If I wasn't honest, I was dubious. At the end of the week, I remembered my scales. I weighed a hundred and twenty-seven.

Exercise, says the *Friend*, will streamline your figure for this spring's fashion favorite. Exercise does not take off weight, but it reduces your measurements. It shifts something, though I can't understand where to.

I was determined not to finish up my diet flabby. Every morning I got up at 6:45 in order to get in some exercising before I was awake.

I'd wake up just in time to find that something had happened to the room. When I'm on my feet, it's plenty big enough. I trip around and never bump into furniture. The moment I "lie on back, arms outstretched at shoulder level, legs together, toes pointed," I cover the whole room. When I "bend knees over chest, drop both knees to floor to right, and stretch legs out without bending knees," I am entangled in the rungs of a chair.

At the end of the fourth week, my waist measurement had decreased by one-sixteenth of an inch, perhaps from the exercise of hopping back into bed. I weighed a hundred and twenty-seven.

There was no help. It had to be calories. Calories also only come in round numbers, by tens. Nothing is seventeen and a half calories.

You need your tape measure for calories, because of things like plums. Two plums, each two and a half inches long, are fifty calories. My plums each measured two inches long. The extra half inch represented one-fifth of a plum, so I was about to eat forty calories. While measuring I got hungry and inadvertently ate a third plum without measuring it. That threw off that day.

The *Friend* is very helpful about calories and publishes lots of low-calorie meals on which people have taken off pounds. You have a different meal every day, and you only buy a half a cup of spinach and six tablespoons of cottage cheese at a time. There are never any leftovers.

I didn't think the *Friend* would want me to throw away good food, so I had to eat up my leftovers first. This meant figuring out exactly how many calories were in them. All the things in calories in the *Friend's* meals are plain things of a definite size and shape. No meat loaf. Too complicated.

To determine how many calories there were in my leftover meat loaf, I had to start from scratch. One ground-round patty two and a half inches in diameter is a hundred calories. I had used a pound, so I bought a new one and divided it all up into two-and-a-half-inch patties. Then I had to take into consideration breadcrumbs, onion, green pepper, a little melted butter, wine. Then it seemed I had made another meat loaf.

At the end of the fifth week, I weighed one hundred and twenty-seven pounds.

All this while, I had cut myself off from my friends. I wanted to surprise them when I emerged, thin, radiant, a new me. But in the sixth week of my dieting, somebody called up, and I didn't know how to get out of it, and then there was a group of people, and we had some drinks, and they *would* go to dinner in a place with spaghetti. I was in *despair*. All my good resolutions were going to be ruined.

But I remembered the *Friend* always said it was *solitary gorging*—those four pieces of bread with mayonnaise (the things some people eat!)—that put on the pounds, because it comforts you for being lonely. And after I had had a few more drinks, I felt pretty popular, and there didn't seem to be any desperate need to change.

The *Friend* was right! I don't remember much about going to bed, but when I struggled onto the scales the next morning I weighed a hundred and twenty-five and a half.

Now I have hopes of a bright new future. If I conscientiously have one party like that every week, I can lose one and a half pounds a week. In four weeks, I will be down to a hundred and twenty-one pounds. If I have two such parties a week—but I'm not sure I can take it. A modest, routine program is what I'm after.

In no time at all I am going to begin to have the rich life the *Friend* promises. If I can do it, you can. I will be popular. I will feel terrific. I will date regularly.

Just as soon as I get through with these parties.

Quit It, Ompremitywise

I FEEL TOLERANT ABOUT ADVERTISING but there is one device of the advertisers that I would like to call their attention to. I think it may get them into trouble.

I am calling this device Omitted Premise Superiority, and, since I am a real American, advertised at regularly, in the flow, the swim, and the drink of our national life, and not an outsider or an egghead (unless you lay the egg flat—my hat size is 23), I am going to be like the advertising copy writers and hereinafter (a word I have always wanted to use) call this device Ompremity.

Here is an example of Ompremity: Gallo wine; picture of lush grapes. "These grapes are only squeezed once."

What, I want to know, is wrong with squeezing grapes twice, or three times, or as many times as it takes to get every bit of juice out of them? There may be a perfectly good reason, such as that if you go on squeezing, you get crushed seeds in your wine. But I want to be told. I don't automatically know why squeezing grapes once is superior.

"The only mustard made with two kinds of specially-grown mustard seed." Why are two kinds of mustard seed better than one? You could sell me just as badly if you said, "The only mustard made with only one specially-grown mustard seed."

"The only cereal with two whole grains." Do all the other cereals have one whole and one half grain? If the bulk were the same, mightn't half grains be easier to chew and not stick in the teeth as much? I'm not questioning the veracity of the statement. I simply want that omitted premise.

Ompremity, as you see, is often associated with the word "only." It is also often associated with a made-up word, as in "the only tooth paste that contains gardol." Gardol and irium and such don't irritate me quite as much, because by their very vagueness they give my inquiring mind something to work on. I can picture to myself some extraordinary substance, a great technical advance, developed in our clean, modern laboratories by a new process, which could certainly do whatever they say it does. My only quarrel with these words is that they aren't alluring. I am told not to buy a chicken unless it is acronized. Does this make my mouth water? Am I yummyized? I'm not, because acronized does not sound like what I would want done to a chicken. It sounds like what I would want done to a hotwater bottle.

Pillsbury tells me that if I use their Hot Roll Mix, I will have the "excitement of working with living dough." What is living dough, and do I want it? Is all dough but Pillsbury's dead? Who's that there in Pillsbury's dough, trying to get out?

If you are not alert, ompremity can trick you into belief. There is a deodorant which is better because it rolls on. At first reading, this seemed to me obvious: of course a deodorant that rolls on is better than one that— well, what? Scrunches in? But mightn't scrunching in be more thorough?

"Roto-roasting" is the "secret that brings out all the golden goodness of the peanuts" used in Big Top peanut butter. (By the way, why is goodness always golden? What about bisque goodness, as in lobster bisque, or chartreuse goodness, as in chartreuse?) Roto comes from the Latin, *rota*, a wheel. Because of having a dictionary, I can get a little further with this ompremity than with most, but I can't get very far. The implication is that these peanuts are roasted on all sides. How do you suppose they do this? Do they spit each peanut with a fine sewing neddle?

The point is that if they don't watch it, the advertisers will be hoist with their own ompremity. I am thinking of the face powder which is proofed against moisture discoloration because it is triple-creamed. I am, as I mentioned above, a regular American, and I have been advertised at to the point where I take it for granted that I am entitled to the very best. Why should I be satisfied with face powder that is only triple-creamed? I want face powder that is at least quintuple-creamed, and now that I think of the very delicate skin I have, I think I should have face powder that is centuple-creamed.

In this country one person is just as special as the next one, except that I am more so. I have just written the *only* article that contains ompremity.

How to Be Happy Though Fired

WHEN I FIRST BEGAN TO JOB hunt I always hoped I wouldn't get the job. I had to nag and bribe myself into office buildings: Go on in, you coward, I would say, go in, you slob, and when you get out you can have coffee and something fattening at the drugstore.

Because whenever I faced a prospective employer the prospect was utterly implausible. Had I been born, lived through chicken pox, measles, adolescence and a B.A. degree to spend the rest of my life in the office of the Better Bundling Blanket Company, shut up with this stranger and concentrating on his or her weird little preoccupations? I would be there forever—or a year, which amounted to the same thing. Could this type across the desk give credence to such a fantastic notion?

This was not conceit. I knew I couldn't do most of the things they expected of me. It made me feel sincerely humble, in fact abysmal. And the last thing they wanted was me. They wanted something else, which, I gathered from reading magazines, was neat and alert in a linen-look, color-secured, Askron-and-Wonderlon, Stretcherized, Testerized, crease-resistant, water-repellent, novelty-weave suit, which wore a light floral cologne and colorless nail polish and washed its hair, its girdle and its powder puff at least once a week. It had written a job-hunting letter saying it wasn't interested in money but in learning about the Better Bundling Blanket Company and how to promote its interests. But they might have to take me for some good reason such as that they weren't offering enough money to get the something else, and if they did, I knew they would gobble me up, snap their jaws shut, and I'd be lost forever.

Psychic states communicate themselves. It was not a bit surprising that without fail I didn't get the job. I helped. When they said, "Do you think you would be able to—?" I said, "No."

Out I would come, knowing I had failed again, happy as a clam in my relentless unemployability.

I might have made a life of never getting jobs if job hunting hadn't been so uncomfortable. It rained. My feet were tired. I had no place to go. People asked me and asked me if I had a job yet. I got broke.

There came a moment when my guard was down. Before I knew it, just like everybody else, I had a job.

The first week is both unbearable and unreal. You don't know what anybody is talking about, or where anything is, or who the people are who call on the telephone who get mad if you don't, and your desk chair snags your stockings, and nobody is ever going to have lunch with you, and there you are, the lowest rung in the Better Bundling Blanket Company, and you are nothing.

Time passes. A certain ease creeps over you. You have a definite place to go when you get up in the morning. You begin to get mildly interested in that special high-ply wool they use in Better Bundling blankets. You're nothing, but so is everyone else.

This might be called Phase Two. Phase Two can last for

years, and many people pass an entire life in it. Employers should do their very best to keep them there, even to getting them new desk chairs.

But sometimes, after a variable lapse of time, you switch to Phase Three. You begin to sense that your original instinct, like most original instincts, was right. Before you got into the Better Bundling Blanket Company you were Jane Doe, nothing special, but yourself. Now you are something else: Miss Doe in the New York Branch, or Miss Doe, J. B.'s secretary, or—the end—Our Miss D. In spite of social security, collective bargaining, and the suggestion box; in spite of clean washrooms, the office Christmas party, and the Billing Department Girls' Bowling Team—your employer owns your soul.

Don't argue. Of course he does. For instance, when does your day start? Not at 7:00, when the alarm rings, but at 5:00 P.M., when you leave the office. It's a very short day, which stops around 10:30, when, in the most uproarious gathering, something begins signaling to you and you realize it is the B.B.B. Co. needing your sleep. There are Saturdays and Sundays? Saturday you wash all those things you're supposed to wash if you're a nice, clean girl—I mean career woman. Sunday is a day of rest, and besides you have all that ironing to do. So they give you a two-week vacation? Anyone who has ever had a two-week vacation knows it is very cleverly timed: it takes at least one week to stop being Our Miss D., and another to get ready to be her again. There's barely time to sandwich a set of tennis in between.

And you really are Our Miss D. You think if you don't get those invoices typed by 4:31; if you don't make that phone call today; if you can't get Our Mr. R. on the afternoon plane to Kansas City—something frightful will happen to the Better Bundling Blanket Company. The B.B.B. Co. is the world and you hold it together. You have to believe this. Otherwise you might surprise yourself wondering who cares whether his blanket is a Better Bundling.

Time and the seasons are passing, and what is the passage of seasons in an office? Spring is Miss Jones, your colleague, just before Easter in a hat incrusted with flowers. Summer is Miss Jones deciding to stop wearing stockings and wondering if she'll bother with leg paint this year. Winter is Miss Jones on the first chill day coming in smelling of moth balls. It's like Plato's cave: life is a shadow on a wall of something going on outside.

In order to develop, a soul needs some privacy in which it can try itself on to see how it looks. An office is the least private place in the world. They know everything. Finding out your age and your salary is elementary—they get those facts the first week, since they're the most important ones. They know what you are giving your grandmother for Christmas, and that you broke your diet and had a chocolate fudge sundae for lunch, that you are fighting with your family, and what you said to the promotion department about what you think of the accounting department. They know all your symptoms of whatever you think you're coming down with—and you know theirs. If you come in wearing dark glasses and a breakable air, they ask if you have a hangover. But they don't need to ask—they know. You can't conceal going to a psychiatrist, even if you go at eight in the morning or six at night, because sometime you'll drop an unguarded "interpersonal relationship" and they'll guess. If you give a party and invite one person from the office, the next day all the others know you didn't invite them. If you think the new man in the advertising department is mildly attractive, they know, and don't think they won't tell him you think he's utterly divine. Then they'll tell you they told him. So before you know whether he's worth a dither, you're in one whenever you see him. This is hysterical love and is to real love as hysterical paralysis is to real paralysis, i.e., all the pain without any of the credit. If the office keeps at you, you may find yourself the mother of the advertising man's three children before you have a chance to realize that this wasn't what you had in mind.

It's unnatural to spend as much time with anyone not related to you as you do with fellow office workers. In one way, they become like relations. Though their interest in your life is avid, you can't surprise them. You hold no mystery for them. If you try to get attention, their reaction is, There's that old shoe flapping its tongue again.

In Phase Three you don't realize all these things immediately and consciously. Its first symptom is a violent loss of interest. For months you've been following the piddling progress of the love life of that other old shoe, Miss Jones. Suddenly you wish she'd stop talking. However juicy, no further detail can enthrall you. You might throw something.

If you can restrain yourself at this point, you'll be safe— in your job. When the sun comes out, or you get over your cold, or Miss Jones starts confiding in someone else, Phase Two will reassert itself, briefly. But from now on you'll zigzag. At the most unexpected moments Phase Three will rear its ugly head. Your fellow workers will feel you restraining yourself from one end of the office to the other.

They will begin to tiptoe. This is the time when you may overhear someone referring to you as "the old fiend."

But if, when you get into Phase Three, you don't restrain yourself; if you throw something or, worse, tell someone something you've been polishing mentally for a month or two—eventually, which is what I am getting to, they will take you out for a couple of regretful Martinis and tell you that they're cutting down your department.

Here—though you won't think so after you've gone home and gloomily had two more Martinis—is the most beautiful moment of your life. Time, which has been racing along in skinny five-and-a-half-hour days, relaxes gloriously into huge, rounded, twenty-four-hour ones. Habits, so fixed that you wondered if you were prematurely old or just getting like your Aunt Susie, become irrelevant and immaterial. Life, losing its focus on Better Bundling blankets, becomes directionless: this means it has a million directions.

You don't have to get up. Half the people in the world love to get up in the morning, and they all work in offices, and this is as it should be. The other half finds getting up so intense a torture that someone should stand by and give them a gold medal every time they make it. I am told this has something to do with one's fluctuations of temperature, so there is a medical reason for it, but the first half thinks the second half is making it up and being difficult. If you are in the second half, and I suspect you are or you wouldn't have been fired, you will experience great bliss. There's one moment of death, when you think you're late to the Better Bundling Blanket Company. Then transfiguration, when you know that you can extend the process of getting up over such a long time that it will be barely perceptible. You can lie there and remember your dreams, and who knows what might come of that? Sometimes you can even go back into them and rearrange them to suit yourself.

You can call your soul your own. For a while you'll call and it won't come: it's mad at you for burying it under Our Miss Doe. But when it sneaks out for a moment or two, don't pounce on it and tell it to go right out and find another job. Let it wander around and see what things are like. It may have entirely different ideas from yours. It doesn't think it's sinful to lie on the sofa and read detective stories all day. It may decide it could write one of its own, entitled *Over the Office Manager's Dead Body.* Or it may start to make an intricate stew that must be stirred every ten minutes. Sometime, when you are walking along the street at three o'clock in the afternoon, your soul will start saying, Oh, joy. Oh, life. Oh, infinite possibilities. This is silly, but why be a spoilsport? Your soul doesn't know what it's doing, but it might find out. It might find out something you lost sight of when you went to work for the Better Bundling Blanket Company: In spite of all the evidence to the contrary, life can change. Even you can change. You may be able to do some of those things Our Miss D. thought were impossible.

People in offices will do everything they can to make you feel that you are living in sin. They telephone at 9:15 A.M. and ask with superior solicitude if they woke you up— they've been up for hours and they'd forgotten you didn't have to be. They wonder if you aren't getting out of the swim. They remark kindly that it's all right for a while, but don't let it become a habit—people can become unemployable. If they come to dinner and eat your stew, they will say that it *is* delicious, but only someone who has all the time in the world could bother with such a thing, and

197

they must tell you the clever trick they've discovered with frozen cheese blintzes. If you visit them in their offices (this is a mistake), they become desperately indispensable: they type memos, telephone, summon messenger boys, ask your pardon for just a moment while they do something rather important, and they only relax when they suggest that with your experience you might be able to get a job at the Woolly Bear Blanket Company, where they know the personnel manager, though it probably wouldn't pay quite as much right away as your old job did.

Let them run on. They have to do something to bolster up their pathetic officebound egos. And you can walk grandly out of there and into the sun, stroll down the street looking in shop windows, watch the seals in the zoo being fed and wonder what it would feel like to be a seal, take a bus ride to a strange part of town, and finally have a nice cup of tea and something fattening in a tearoom.

What does this remind you of? If I were you I wouldn't think about it. You're not going to make the same mistake again, are you? Or are you?

Picking Your Mate with a Menu

LIKES AND DISLIKES OF FOOD HAVE always been considered inexplicable, pleasantly uncharted oddities and a part of personality. But, as it must to all oddities, comes (alas) an explanation. According to Dr. William Kaufman, a doctor in Bridgeport, Connecticut, one's likes and dislikes are based on the emotional values of food. Dr. Kaufman has established some interesting categories, which I like because they offer a new way of getting the jump on other people.

The first category is security foods—milk and milk products. We increase our intake of these in times of emotional stress. Mother is involved here.

There are reward foods—chocolate, hot dogs, candy, or nuts. We eat more of these "if we are thwarted, or if we have failed to gain the approval of others, or if we feel sorry for ourselves."

Fetish foods include things like highly advertised cereals, which we eat more of "if we need extra strength to compete successfully with others. Some children don't feel strong unless they have Wheaties, Breakfast of Champions; some adults believe they can't sleep without first taking Ovaltine. Many laborers feel that if deprived of daily servings of red meat and potatoes, they would become too weak to work."

Grown-up foods include coffee, tea, or beer, and are fa-

199

vored by people who "have the unconscious need to emphasize their adulthood."

There are pleasurable-association foods: "When we are
sad or lonely, we may have special need to recapture sym-
bolically some treasured moments of past happiness." Dr.
Kaufman gives as an example "baked beans, which remind
us of our beloved Aunt Clarissa."

Show-off foods are another category. People who, says
Dr. Kaufman, "are impelled to attract the attention of
others . . . may eat odd things such as live goldfish . . .
or fried grasshoppers. . . . Others more modest in their
aspirations may prefer to establish local reputations by
gorging themselves publicly on watermelon, clams, pump-
kin pie, or hamburgers. The less imaginative . . . merely
splash generous amounts of ketchup, mustard, or black pepper over everything they eat."

Prestige foods include "caviar, truffles, expensive but
smelly cheeses, and dry champagne of a certain vintage
year."

There are also foods to which people have "unfavorable
emotional reactions," for example, those with built-in con-
flicts, which were "the original 'parent-fight-child' foods,
such as spinach and carrots." Then there are foods that
produce "unfavorable emotional reactions," including, not
surprisingly, "spoiled foods, off-color foods, off-taste foods."

This may seem complicated at first. For instance, as long
as it is cheap and doesn't smell, cheese is a security food.
Smelly and expensive—prestige. Red meat is a fetish food,
yet hamburgers are show-off, which seems to indicate it is
the hamburger bun which is intrinsically exhibitionist. The
truffles are also confusing. I have always understood that

the true truffle lovers were truffle hounds or hogs. Possibly they want prestige, too.

But the complications are worth facing up to and even delving into because they present such enthralling possibilities. Having a meal in a restaurant with someone else has heretofore been a social occasion in which guarded or unguarded confidences might or might not be exchanged. Now, willy-nilly, masks will drop. This is going to be most helpful when you are lunching or dining with a strange young man, a circumstance, owing to obsession with one's own mask, in which it is harder than usual to assess character. It is also a situation on which a good deal of advice has been given over the ages, but nobody except Dr. Kaufman has advised noting what the other person orders. Spying like this may seem underhand if you are not a doctor, but in this age of security-consciousness, it is a good idea to collect every crumb of information you can.

Well, here are a few indications of how to go about it. Suppose your date orders Welsh rabbit, containing cheese and beer. Presumably the cheese was relatively cheap and not smelly, so it is a security food. The beer is grown-up. This means he wants to emphasize that he is an adult, but the whole thing upsets him. Pretend you think he is an adult, too.

He gaily commandeers some American champagne. He wants to show off, but doesn't have the courage of his convictions. An essentially cautious type (maybe even stingy), so be careful yourself.

He has a chocolate fudge sundae with salted almonds. This indicates a serious personality problem. Note that he has rewarded himself twice. He is feeling doubly sorry for himself, because of his insecurity. Maybe you should stop showing off.

He puts ketchup on his baked beans. He wants to recapture that wonderful moment when he showed off, and Aunt Clarissa was sympathetic. This is encouraging—you have made an impression.

He has pot cheese with sour cream. You will be surprised, but this is a Don Juan. Note that he chooses a double security food. As you doubtless know, Don Juans are very insecure people who have a constant need to prove themselves. Watch out.

He has a little Roquefort cheese. He has been under emotional stress so long that it's beginning to spoil. This person doesn't get any fun out of telling how awful everything is, but tells it anyway so you won't get any fun out of it, either. I would advise steering clear.

But if he orders New England clam chowder, he is showing off about his troubles. He is, consequently, more extroverted, and you may go happily down the years together hand in hand with his emotional stress.

He has red meat cooked with wine. Either he has a fetish about being a snob, or is a snob about fetishes. New England boiled dinner was good enough for his grandmother. Fun to play with, but won't get serious.

He orders a big bowl of a highly advertised dry cereal with milk or cream. He has a fetish about being under stress. Of course, there is a possibility that he wants to send for a set of five scale-model plastic Fords, or an atomic beanie. Consider whether he might not be too young for you.

He has coffee ice cream. He is very split, trying to be an adult and heading back to the womb at the same time. This type may also be too young for you.

Creamed spinach. He is fighting with his mother. Take his side, cautiously.

Chocolate cake with whipped cream. He is feeling sorry for himself because he wants to beat up his mother. This does not look good.

Crème renversée. He wants to turn his mother upside down. Worse.

Crème brûlée. Very bad. Run.

That will do for a starter. In any case, you have only a day or two in which to put this into effect, because as soon as everyone knows about it, people will start choosing foods in reverse, and the real snobs will take care to order glasses of milk. And they'll begin watching you.

How to Mend a Broken Heart

THIS IS A COUNTRY WHERE EVERYTHING IS housed except the heart. Its geography is the same as that of the county now lost, but distorted as if by a mirage. Persistently the heart pays its ghostly visits to familiar landmarks, and finds them strange: they have assumed extra and unbearable significances. Jammed to the bleachers, the Yankee Stadium may be a graveyard. The gold curtain of the Metropolitan Opera House falls, not on the end of the opera, but on hope. The lions in front of the Public Library have ceased to be arrogant: they are about to roar with woe.

Time in this country is extraordinarily long. Much of it is passed in silently directing across the frontier an endless letter of protest and explanation, rage and tenderness. The letter is most eloquent late at night, and sometimes spoken out loud. It cannot rest with something said once, but marks its ocean of hours with recurrent and identical tides.

The other people in this country are unreal and yet troubling. Laughter in the street is a stab; a couple holding hands a mortal wound. Happy, people are a reproach or an affront. Miserable, they don't know the half of it. Unkind, they confirm your conviction that you are not worth the world's consideration for a moment. Kind, they demonstrate the heart-rending discrepancy which exists between kindness and love.

The only person who could give comfort is the one who caused the desolation. What is there to do but lie on the sofa and cry? No other pursuit could dignify the catastrophe. Except death.

Inexplicably and annoyingly, one doesn't die.

Those most interested in this article—the broken-hearted —are about to protest that they very well may. Who, they are thinking, is this superficial wordmonger, who believes feelings like mine can be transitory? Nothing so bad has ever happened before. I will never get over it.

This is a most old-fashioned state of mind. "Broken-hearted" sounds dated. "Unrequited" seems to belong to a period of steel engravings of weeping willows, preferably growing aslant brooks. "Crossed in love" has the flavor of an even earlier time: it suggests consolingly that stars, gods, some powerful agency outside oneself, have had a hand in the situation.

We have pushed morality further than did people of previous generations, even stuffy ones. Today, one must feel responsible for what happens. Having a broken heart is culpable: you have probably done something wrong. "It is normal to overidealize a beloved person," says Dr. Smiley Blanton in *Love or Perish*, "and so make more valuable the object of our heart's desire." But people who overidealize make excessive demands which "inevitably reach a point where they must be met with refusal." "*Don't*," he says in his own italics, "*give your love to those who cannot return it!*" To do so "perpetuates infantile patterns of self-delusion and unfits us for effective dealing with our fellow men."

"Perpetuating infantile patterns of self-delusion" is distinctly more modern than being broken-hearted. If your

How to Mend a Broken Heart

heart has been breached, contemporary advisers will not rush in with comfort and remedies. "Why," they are more likely to ask, "did you do it in the first place?" To find the answer may lead one into a complete and professional overhaul of the personality.

Writers of earlier ages, who never heard of such therapy, assumed that heartbreak happened, that the cure might be long and difficult, but that certain courses of action could be helpful. If one does not have the money for a complete overhaul, they are worth consulting. They knew exactly how you feel: if you insist belligerently on being out-of-date, you will find them more satisfactory than the twentieth-century advisers.

Stendhal describes falling in love as "crystallization," because of the phenomenon he observed in the Salzburg salt mines: if you throw a bare branch into a pit and fish it out two or three months later, you find the branches covered with crystals. The smallest twig is a mass of sparkling diamonds, and the original is no longer recognizable. In love, crystallization is "the work of the spirit which draws from everything that confronts it the discovery that the loved object has new perfections." This is better. It may be infantile, but it sounds charming.

How does one decrystallize? Stendhal, in De l'amour, Robert Burton, in The Anatomy of Melancholy, and Ovid, in Remedia Amoris, give the broken-hearted advice on all the concerns of the waking day and many of those of the night, and their advice is practical. Occasionally it requires a little translation, but not much. If one must suffer, to suffer with Ovid (three wives and at least one Corinna) establishes something that has seemed doubtful: one is still a part of the human race.

"Labour, slender and sparing diet, with continual business," says Burton, "are the best and most ordinary means to prevent [love-melancholy]." For many, this will ring a bell, those who have a strong natural overhaul instinct of their own, those, that is, who are listmakers. Listmakers yearn toward ascetism: they live, mentally fingering resolutions, as if every day were New Year's.

If you are a listmaker and broken-hearted, you will translate Burton for yourself and begin a new list, the one which goes something like this: "Get up at quarter of eight sharp. Only three cigarettes before lunch. No hard liquor before six or after dinner. Lose ten pounds by August 21. Do not telephone X. Make new friends. Read twenty pages of *War and Peace* every day. No salted peanuts." You write this in a beautifully formed hand, and sit back to contemplate the clean positiveness of your personality on paper. How controlled, how superior you are to all the irresolute!

Unfortunately, listmakers are by definition listbreakers. Knowing this, they are ashamed of being listmakers and conceal it like a secret vice. But the company is distinguished. Consider this list, and what happened to it.

For the 15th. From 5 to 8, writing; from 8 to 9, music and tea; from 9 to 11, gymnastics; from 11 to 1, reduce to a certain order my affairs before my departure, but without hurrying. From 1 to 10, luncheon, writing, reading and a walk.

April 15th. Rose late—at 8 o'clock. *Sloth* and *indecision.* Did gymnastics well, played the piano *with haste,* read *similarly,* dined with my aunt and disputed with her. *Lack of fierté.* After dinner, spent evening in prowling about and experiencing *voluptuous* desires.

Listmakers like italics. This one is Tolstoi in 1851.

The danger of making lists while broken-hearted is the danger of doing anything you have done before while broken-hearted—intensification. If you don't stick to your list, you will feel even more worthless, and you feel quite worthless already.

But if you feel you cannot stick to the list, do not give yourself up. "If they be much dejected and brought low in body, and now ready to despair through anguish, grief, and too sensible a feeling of their misery, a cup of wine and full diet is not amiss." In other words, "Stay me with flagons, comfort me with apples; for I am sick of love." Or in still other words, if each day is a tissue of dreary tasks extending into the limp and dangling fringe of a lonely evening, go ahead and have a dry Martini or two, and a delicious dish of noodles and cheese, representing seven hundred calories.

But the seven hundred calories remain a problem. It is a mystery to me why the unrequited lovers of literature and the past were pale, wan, and thin, while nowadays emotional troubles lead to overeating. Either something has changed radically or pining away is a literary convention. From reading Burton, I suspect that the latter is possible. The slender and sparing diet he recommends consists of "Cowcumbers, Melons, Water-Lilies, Rue, Woodbine, Ammi, Lettis," a salad unquestionably low in calories. I think he knew someone with a broken heart, who was out in the larder gorging on suckling pig and saddle of mutton.

What can one do? The only answer I can think of is to solace oneself with something very small that will take time to make—one cracker with a little grated cheese on it

209

and half a rolled anchovy in the middle toasted very slowly under the broiler, and topped with a sprinkle of rue.

For the unrequited, strong drink may be nectar, balm, and the only thing to look forward to. Ovid's unexpected advice is not to drink, but if you must, to get plastered: "Either let there be no drunkenness, or to so great an extent to remove your anxieties; if there is any medium between the two it is injurious." There is something to be said for this: a blow-up can have the effect of shifting the gears and a hangover may be so absorbing that you forget your troubles. Perhaps Ovid is thinking of the hangover when he says: "That you may recover, you will have to endure much that is to be lamented."

There are people who are never excessive, who never need to make lists. There are such people, though I have trouble formulating them in my mind. In general, they are satisfied with themselves: listmakers wish to change and be better. But the satisfied, too, are subject to the broken heart. While they may not have the problem of wondering what they did wrong, they face the basic one: the boundless loneliness which is like the dark around a fire out of doors. For a while it can be pushed back, but it always looms.

Everything is related to the person who has forced one into this loneliness. The only way to make it bearable seems to be to hope for a return: to watch for the mail, listen for the telephone, and live continually in the expectation of the encounter. You know better and so does Ovid: "Let not that portico which is wont to receive her as she walks receive you as well," he says, which means, do not be walking down Madison Avenue past his office at five minutes past five.

With all such desires to return to the past, he is severe.

"Nor yet, though you should desire to know, should you ask how she is doing." "Take care not to read over again the letters that you have kept. . . . Put the whole of them into the devouring flames." "Remove her waxen portrait as well."

And finally, go away. "Neither do you count the hours, nor oft look back on Rome: but fly." And stay away at least a year, adds Burton, some sixteen hundred years later.

Here there is an interesting divergence between the authorities. Though the prescription for travel is time-honored, Stendhal does not agree. Stendhal enjoyed being a tender soul, and what he called trembling. His love-melancholy was stubborn; he half enjoyed it, and half doubted it could be cured. The lonely journey, he says, is not a remedy: nothing recalls more tenderly what one loves than contrasts. Therefore if one goes away, one must go with a friend, the curing friend (l'ami guérisseur), who, says Stendhal subtly, should talk incessantly about the unfortunate love affair to the point where it bores the bereaved to distraction.

Traveling is expensive nowadays, and so is another time-honored prescription: meet new people ("Fly not from conversation, nor let your door be closed"). Meeting new people means parties. To be invited to parties one must give them, and it would be nice to have a new dress for the occasion. All the old ones hang limply at half-mast in mourning for past occasions. Perhaps such diversions were cheaper in the old days. Now it comes down to money. If you have it, you may stop reading me (but take Stendhal, Burton, or Ovid with you) and go out and buy a new wardrobe and a steamship ticket.

But you haven't. Assuming a broken heart, reading is almost the only thing I can think of that costs nothing. It is certainly much better than prowling about and experiencing voluptuous desires. The ancients have considered this also. "Meddle not with the amorous poets," says Ovid, and he goes on to emphasize the importance of this by advising the unrequited not to read Ovid. "Even my own lines have tones indescribably sweet." Joyous love poetry will make you grieve, and the sad will express that grief. Most of the good love poems, with a few exceptions, are by men. If you are a woman, reading them will make you feel not only unrequited, but unchronicled. Where possible avoid Romantic poets, cultivate Classical ones. Byron is an exception in the first case; Catullus in the second.

Humorous verse is preferable, and bad verse (in small doses) is almost as good, since it makes unrequited love ridiculous. For example, from Tottel's *Miscellany* (1557):

> Farewell, thou frozen heart and ears of
> hardened steel,
> Thou lackest years to understand the grief
> that I did feel.

Do not, says Ovid, "indulge yourself with the Theatres, until Love has entirely departed from your liberated breast. The harps, and the pipes, and the lyres, soften the feelings; the voices, too. . ." This seems to preclude the opera and is probably wise unless the opera is carefully chosen. *La Bohème* and *Madame Butterfly* are out; *Tosca* is doubtful; *Così fan tutte* is better. Though the *Marriage of Figaro* is ideal in many ways, the Contessa is a hazard: "Porgi amor," which ends with the classic "At least let me die," and "Dove sono i bei momenti," will make you cry.

Indulging nostalgically in popular songs is, of course, nothing but indulgence.

The third and fourth of the arts, painting and sculpture, are, because of their present depersonalization, by far the safest. Somewhere in the galleries you may run into an abstraction called "Broken Heart," but it is unlikely to unnerve you.

These are distractions: what advice does the past offer about the attitude of mind which will be most efficacious?

The past, with wisdom, is chary about any, knowing that in this condition it is impossible to assume an attitude through an effort of the will. The broken-hearted feels there has been an exposure and isolation of his personality. A strange instinct tells him that the exposure is both true and false. Such ambivalent states of mind are endlessly instructive, but they make taking an attitude almost impossible.

In so far as the exposure seems false, rage is possible. Here the curing friend is again recommended, to point out all the things to which you have been blind: "Odd relationship with his mother," "Awful to his first wife," "Why do you suppose he butters his bread like that?" and so on. "Let all these points ferment through your entire feelings; repeat them over and over; hence seek the first germs of your hate." "Tell him but how he was scoffed at behind his back," says Burton, and gives a magnificent and terrifying list of the things the rejecter has supposedly said about the rejected one. If this does not work, he advises "good counsel": that "in sober sadness, marriage is a bondage, a thraldom, a yoke, an hindrance to all good enterprises, a stop to all preferments."

Then both writers, perhaps momentarily afflicted with the half-sweet longing familiar to tender souls, contradict themselves. "Marriage," says Burton, "is the last and best

213

refuge and cure of Heroical love." "Tis a crime," says Ovid, "to hate the fair one so lately loved; such a termination as that is befitting a brutal disposition." So what does one do? Can one detach one's love from the object, make it more general, more pervasive, and so keep it? This would be the ideal solution, but no one says whether and how it is possible.

For a tender soul, that half-sweet longing is the climate in which another affection might blossom. Love, like nature, abhors a vacuum. The final advice is that the best way to get over a broken heart is to risk starting the whole thing over again by falling in love with someone else.

You are caught. You must remain old-fashioned. "Every passion is conquered by a fresh successor." Who has ever had a broken heart about the next to last person?

Yawp for Today

TODAY I AM NOT MAD AT ANYONE. THE vernal equinox has arrived. The sun is out. My window is open, and through it wafts grinding, chugging, blasting, and riveting from the corner, where they are building an apartment house.

In what other country would something you pay a great deal of money first to own and then to maintain be called—cooperative?

In spite of what I have said elsewhere, I love gadgets. I love American ingenuity. It is not ingenious alone, but extravagant and precise. American ingenuity can be as baroque as a bibelot, and as functional as a fly swatter.

Today I have no wish to carp. Today I shall harp. Gadgets I sing. I have just realized who I am today—Walt Whitman. I too can sound a barbaric yawp over the roofs of the world. Today a rude brief recitative.

Come Muse, migrate from Greece and Ionia, because in what other country would they suggest that the suitable memorial gift to your church or your alma mater is a set of Schulmerich Carillonic Bells? How endlessly rocking these bells, enduring in beauty, practical in price, efficient in installation, simple in maintenance, and, of course, tax-deductible.

Have the elder races halted? Do they droop and end their

215

lesson, wearied over there beyond the seas? They do, because in Europe the flints you buy for your lighter come in a little paper envelope, and here we have Zip-a-flint by Zippo. Here are flints in a row in a little plastic tube, and here at the end is a small red wheel with a mouth. How precisely the mouth gobbles exactly one flint. How modestly it presents it to you! You who celebrate bygones, who have explored the outward, the surfaces of the races, the life that has exhibited itself, you historians and archaeologists, what an impossible task in future times will you have trying to figure out what Zip-aflint by Zippo was for. O something ecstatic and undemonstrable!

There are some days when Univac scares me, but not today. Today I think I could live with Univac—it is so placid and self-contained. It does not lie awake in the dark and weep for its sins. It does not make me sick discussing its duty to God. It just sits there and grinds out a concordance to the Bible.

In the labor of engines and trades, I find the developments. I find the zippered doily file of see-through plastic, the pleatmaster kit, and the decorative switch plates. I find the noiseless patient dripless candle, after long years and trying developed. And I find that someone feeling deprived of drips has invented the Cascade Candle, which drips on purpose. It launches forth filament, filament, filament, out of itself, ever unreeling them, ever tirelessly speeding them all down its solid and colorful sides.

Mark the spirit of invention everywhere, thy rapid patents. The responsibility of gadgets! How calm they are, how kind and how thoughtful. My roll of waxed paper is vigilant. As it comes toward its end, it worries. It tells me in neatly punched letters: "Time to reorder Cut-Rite." Yet it knows I am fallible, human, forgetful, and it is indulgent. It says it again and again until I reorder.

Buying a box of vitamins, I found there a paper, a gift and remembrancer designedly dropt. I have never met you, friend, but I feel that I know you. You wish me well, and I you, and you send me this ensign of duty. The small piece of paper tells me: "Packed by Clock No. 398."

We pass through Kanada, the Northeast, the vast valley of the Mississippi, and the Southern states, and everywhere we find the same toaster, identical, shiny, and modular, which pops up two pieces of toast. And through all these regions, it cannot toast corn or bran muffins. O the engineer's joys—they invent new muffins, and these you can toast. *These* are toaster-tailored.

What unknown hero defined the erasers, assigned them their tasks, and displayed them that now we may have job-mated erasers?

We do not blame thee elder World, nor really separate ourselves from thee, but have you ever conceived of a stove with a built-in meat thermometer, which you stick in the roast and, when it is done, the thermometer plays a tune, and the tune is "Tenderly." The muse is here, install'd amid the kitchenware!

Hurrah for positive science! Long live exact demonstration! O, tumble-dried! O, packaged plumbing! O, pilferproof closure! Melange mine own, for I too am job-mated. I am toaster-tailored. I am integral with you, I too am of one phase and of all phases. I am America, and today I dote on myself, there is that lot of me, and all so luscious.

How Did This Happen?

NOTE: When I wrote about Lady Mondegreen in what a correspondent tells me was always *Papa's* magazine, I did not realize how many people knew as much about Lady Mondegreen as I did. Reading their letters, I saw that Lady Mondegreen's death was only the beginning. I am not one to tell you not to put beans up your nose, so I will not suggest that you will not understand *The Quest of Lady Mondegreen* unless you have read *The Death of Lady Mondegreen* on page 105 first.

Some people wrote to correct me, but as before, this is a question of who is to be master. If there is a word, it is the word, but if there is more than one mondegreen, it is Lady Mondegreen. Harold's name is Harold, not Hallowell or Halibut, both of which are of too narrowly New England a character. The argument for Halibut was that the early Christians identified themselves by the sign of the fish. Harold does not belong solely to the early Christian era.

Some people felt I had done Harold a disservice by so identifying him. It comes down to attributes. If he has none whatsoever, he cannot be permitted to walk in the garden in the cool of the day, which seems unkind. If he has attributes, may I not name a few? They are not exclusive: I will name them on Choosedays, and leave everyone else the rest of the week.

All the readers who made contributions to these further or before-the adventures must forgive me if I do not thank them personally and mention their names. I have taken it for granted that they gave me their mondegreens with nose rings attached. Thus they will be able to identify their own.

The Quest of Lady Mondegreen

ONCE UPON THE TIME BEFORE THINGS got going Lady Mondegreen and Good Mrs. Murphy lived together in Tizzathee.

Tizzathee was a splendid country. Above Tizzathee were not one, as elsewhere, but (Oh, beautiful!) four spacious skies. The sunsets and sunrises in 4–D were extraordinary.

The people in Tizzathee enjoyed themselves. After the day's work, they sat around in the evening and heard the latest songs on the Hip Hooray. It is true that some of them worked themselves up by listening to the End-of-the-World Series. But even these went to bed serene, because they knew they would be guarded by Babe Ruth through the night.

Lady Mondegreen climbed the rocks, slid down the sand rills, and wandered in the woods. She had not thought of any questions to ask.

Good Mrs. Murphy had long ago answered all the questions to her satisfaction, and she was busy in the kitchen and other places.

Tizzathee is the land of liver tea, which is full of itemends, is good for you, and has a strong taste of nothing. Tizzathee is also one nation and a vegetable, which has a weak taste of nothing. Twice a day, when Lady Mondegreen sat down to lunch and dinner, a vegetable appeared, fortified, homogenized, defrosted, and neatly prepared by Good Mrs. Murphy. Lady Mondegreen did not like it, but Good Mrs. Murphy had brought her up properly and she knew she had to eat it. So she prayed to Harold to help her. Twice a day, she said, "Incline our hearts to eat this slaw."

One day, something in Tizzathee was different. The four skies may have been a little more spacious, the Hip Hooray a little more specious, or a vegetable a little more tasteless. Whatever it was, for the first time Lady Mondegreen wondered. She found it a little painful, but absorbing.

Toward evening, she knew what she was wondering about and went into the kitchen to consult Good Mrs. Murphy, who was brewing a pot of liver tea on the back of the old black stove.

Good Mrs. Murphy looked suspiciously at her over her shoulder. "You look peaked," she said. "Have you been eating something you shouldn't?"

This confirmed Lady Mondegreen's wondering. "You never told me before that there was anything I shouldn't eat," she said.

"I can't do everything in this house," said Good Mrs. Murphy. "And I wouldn't be one to advise you not to put beans up your nose." She had been saving this one up. It was a drastic distraction, but she saw that something drastic was needed.

It didn't work. "Where is fancy bread?" asked Lady Mondegreen.

Good Mrs. Murphy sat down heavily in the kitchen rocker. "Who told you about fancy bread?" she asked. "Have you been talking to any snakes?"

"It came to me," said Lady Mondegreen, "and I want some. I'm sick of a vegetable."

"It's a bad, bad thing," said Good Mrs. Murphy, shaking her head. "You'll be getting nightmares and notions and going off exploring. You're better off without it."

"How can I be once I've thought of it?" said Lady Mondegreen.

"If you must, you must," said Good Mrs. Murphy gloomily. "But you'll live to wish you'd listened to kind old Good Mrs. Murphy. Oh, you'll enjoy yourself for a while no doubt, but there will come a moment when you'll say to yourself, Why didn't I pay more mind to wise old Good Mrs. Murphy? There'll come a time—"

By now, Lady Mondegreen knew she would get what she wanted, so she kissed Good Mrs. Murphy and went out into the yard to think about how fancy bread would taste.

That evening, with many sighs, Good Mrs. Murphy placed before her for dessert a delicious small brown loaf, topped with white frosting. Lady Mondegreen beamed at it, cut a slice, and ate it.

No thunder or anything else dramatic clapped. The fancy bread tasted better than Lady Mondegreen had imagined. That seemed to be all. Lady Mondegreen sat back in her chair.

"I am a mondegreen," she said, discovering.

"Why yes, my dear," said Good Mrs. Murphy, relieved. "Aren't we all?"

"There are other mondegreens?" asked Lady Mondegreen. "I feel like the first one."

"I knew you'd get ideas in your head," said Good Mrs. Murphy. "You're no different from the next one. And if I had my way I'd keep the next one out of here."

223

But Lady Mondegreen had already gone to answer the knock at the back door.

Three of them were standing outside, all about the same size. The first was a plump boy, the second an alert-looking camel, and the third a cinnamon-colored bear with shoe-button eyes sewn on crooked. She motioned them to come into the kitchen.

"These are my friends," she said to Good Mrs. Murphy.

"It's not enough to have to beat up fancy bread at a moment's notice," said Good Mrs. Murphy. "Now I have to pick up after camels and bears and boys. And don't just stand there. Sit down properly at the table and say your names. Only one piece of fancy bread apiece, mind you."

"Round John Virgin," said the boy, bowing.

"O Camel, the Faithful," said the camel, eyeing the fancy bread.

"Gladly," said the bear.

"Tell your name nicely," said Good Mrs. Murphy, firmly.

"Gladly," he said apologetically, "the cross-eyed bear."

They all sat down around the table and began to eat fancy bread. Lady Mondegreen looked at them purposefully.

"We have to get up early tomorrow," she said, "to make a good start."

"Where are we going?" asked Round John Virgin.

"To find the Earl Amurray," she said.

"Earls is it now?" said Good Mrs. Murphy. "I knew no good would come of this."

"I will come," said O Camel, "since I am for company. Company is for comment. Must we look for an earl? I would rather look for more fancy bread."

"Don't come looking here," said Good Mrs. Murphy.

"Once in a way for a treat, but not as a steady diet. A nice cup of liver tea is what you'll get for breakfast."

"Mondegreens don't like liver tea," said Lady Mondegreen, "and have earls to find."

"Now she has no more use for poor old Good Mrs. Murphy," said poor old Good Mrs. Murphy. "Now she has her fine friends and her fine ideas. All for nothing have I done for her all these years."

"You make the best fancy bread in the whole world," said Lady Mondegreen.

"It's the recipe my mother brought from the old country," said Good Mrs. Murphy. "You won't find its like here."

"I will go, too," said Round John Virgin. "Since I am for finding out about things. What is a knoll country? What is a mondegreen?"

"The questions the child asks," said Good Mrs. Murphy. "Only the Good Harold could answer them."

They all looked at Gladly.

"What are you for?" asked Round John Virgin.

"I don't know," said Gladly, ducking his head with embarrassment. "I don't see myself well. Could I be for coming too?"

"Don't fuss the bear," said Good Mrs. Murphy. "Why should he know what he's for? Take things as they come, I always say. And no more talk. If you want to be fresh in the morning, to bed with you."

They awoke the next morning to a nellaparting day, which looks as if it were about to be over when it has just begun. But, invigorated by their steaming liver tea, they decided to start anyway. They said good-by to Good Mrs. Murphy, who gave them a great deal of advice and rubbers, and they set out.

They took the usual road out of Tizzathee, which is always wet ahead of you but dries as you get there. They crossed the fruited plain, climbed over the four purple mountains, and arrived in another country. Here there was a crossroads with four roads leading out of it. A signpost directed as follows:

TO THE SANDS OF D

TO THE BARREN WASTE

TO THE SOFT DANCER

FROM SEA TO CHINA SEA

They stopped to consider the sign.

"Secrets," said Lady Mondegreen.

"Then there's nothing to do but count out," said O Camel.

Lady Mondegreen closed her eyes, and they turned her around several times. She said a counting-out rhyme which had just occurred to her:

> Barren sands, waste sea,
> Soft to China,
> Dance to D,
> One, two, three,
> Out.

When she opened her eyes, she was pointing to TO THE SANDS OF D.

"Exactly the one I wanted," said Gladly.

They started down the road which lead to the Sands of D, which went and turned and went and twisted until they came to the edge of a wide sandy beach. Blue water shimmered far away on the other side.

"I almost know what we do here," said Lady Mondegreen.

"Quiet for cogitation," said O Camel. She thought.

"Here we call the cattalome," she said finally.

"Of course," said O Camel, "It was tipping my tongue."

They lined up in a row and called until in the distance they saw the cattalome coming slowly across the sand.

The cattalome was a large, shapeless, sand-colored beast, with a flipperlike fin on each side with which it propelled itself. This was both awkward and slow, so it encouraged itself by saying over and over in a deep, rasping voice, "Get along, cattalome, get along, cattalome." The cattalome's mother liked railroad trains.

When it arrived in front of them, it looked up inquiringly from under a thick fold of flesh that served it as eyebrows, and said, "Yes."

"How do you get along?" said Lady Mondegreen. This is how you greet a cattalome.

"Fin, thank you," said the cattalome politely. "And you?"

"I am looking for the Earl Amurray," said Lady Mondegreen. "Do you know where he is?"

"You're not to ask me questions," said the cattalome.

"Why not?" asked Round John Virgin.

"Because one question leads to another," it said crossly. "I am to be called and that is all. Not on or for. Called. Everyone has to call occasionally, and I could be useful to them because I don't commit them to anything. But they all have to ask questions. They can't let well enough reason for being alone."

"Is there only one reason for being alone?" asked Round John Virgin.

"I am a cattalome," it said. "If I did anything but be called, I'd stop being it." Its jowly face became lugubrious. "I would be something else. That scares me."

227

"Are you a mondegreen?" asked Round John Virgin.

"Now stop it," said the cattalome, "but since you asked, certainly not. A mondegreen is a stray. A cattalome may occasionally be distrait, never astray. A cattalome stands pat."

"—alone," finished O Camel, and he snorted to himself. The cattalome wrinkled its eyebrow alarmingly.

"Thank you very much," said Lady Mondegreen. "I think we must be going."

"Earls are chancy," said the cattalome. "You won't find any here. Steer clear of them." It turned slowly around and flopped cumbersomely off, muttering urgently to itself, "Paddle home, cattalome, paddle home, cattalome."

They returned to the crossroads.

Lady Mondegreen counted out again. She couldn't remember exactly how it had gone the first time, so this time she said:

> Soft sea, barren sea
> Shining waste,
> Dance to three,
> One, two,
> Out.

And this time she pointed to TO THE SOFT DANCER.

"I was hoping for that one," said Gladly.

"Let us think it over," said O Camel, sitting down judiciously at the side of the road. "Could the cattalome be right? Do we want to find a chancy earl? Nobody asked me, of course, but I think we should use our heads on this problem."

"He's only chancy until we find him," said Lady Mondegreen. "We're a quarter of the way there already, and we'll soon be halfway if we don't loaf."

228   *The Quest of Lady Mondegreen*

"I'm only half loafing," said O Camel, "and half a loaf is better than no head. I have to be faithful, but you wouldn't notice it if I didn't inject a little objection."

"Now that you've objected, can we go?" said Round John Virgin.

"I'll just set back for a moment longer," said O Camel, "Every quest must have a setback."

They waited until O Camel felt he had set back long enough, and then set off again.

The second path led immediately into a vast pine forest. It bent and turned and bent and twisted and they walked happily along, dry pine needles crunching under their feet, hoping to see the soft dancer at any moment.

So they were extremely shocked when suddenly there was a loud explosion, and a terrifying figure leaped out from the depths of the wood. It was as tall as the tallest pine, and covered with fire darting out in every direction. Its face grinned fearfully down at them, and its teeth were pointed flames. It held a glittering cage with which it lunged at them.

"I have read of Fiery Gasful with his burnished rows of steel," gasped Lady Mondegreen, "and this must be he." She turned to run.

"Impossible, preposterous, outrageous," shouted Fiery Gasful, exploding like a bomb on each explosive. "I won't have it. I won't stand for it. I hate it."

They all began to run as Fiery Gasful continued to explode behind them. After they had gone a little distance there was a sudden silence.

They looked around and saw that Fiery Gasful had stopped dead, and was flaring at a willowy lady, who was dancing slowly out of the woods. She had long pale hair and she wore a pale floating dress.

"Blast, blast, blast," yelled Fiery Gasful, and did. That is, he blew up and vanished. Everything was quiet and empty, except that a few ashes floated slowly down, settling here and there, on the grass, on pine needles, and in the hair of the willowy lady.

She did not trouble to brush them out, but lay languidly down on the grass.

Lady Mondegreen approached her. "You're the soft dancer that turneth away wrath," she said.

"I suppose so," said the lady, "My name is Mildly Lazy Gloraby."

"What an odd name," said Round John Virgin, who had never thought about his own. "Why are you mildly lazy?"

"Too much of an effort to be violently lazy," she said.

"Are you a mondegreen?" he asked.

"Not if I can help it," said Mildly Lazy Gloraby. "A mondegreen is a motion, and I make as few motions as possible."

"Have you seen the Earl Amurray?" asked Lady Mondegreen.

"If I had, I wouldn't know him," she said. "I'm indifferent. You all look alike to me."

"What's different?" asked Round John Virgin.

"I don't know," she said. "I'm in it. I can't see it for the trees." She yawned, turned over, and went to sleep.

"Do you think she has any fancy bread?" asked Gladly in a whisper.

"If she had, she wouldn't know it," said Round John Virgin disgustedly.

"I would too," said Mildly Lazy Gloraby, opening one

eye. "I already ate it." This time she really went to sleep.

"I like it here," said Gladly. "Let's take a nap, too. She might have more fancy bread when she wakes up."

"I thought you were for coming along too," said O Camel.

"I am," he said. "I'm for coming along too with everybody. Not for choices. I don't like it when we leave people behind."

"She's not going anywhere, and we are," said Round John Virgin.

"I like them both," said Gladly.

"We could leave you behind," said Round John Virgin.

"We can't do that," said O Camel. "Someone on this quest has to accept things unconditionally, so that the rest of us can be on-condition-that. Let's sit down and figure this out. Every quest should have a rest."

They lay down on the pine needles in a patch of sunlight.

"Lovely," said Gladly.

"Are you enjoying it to the full?" said O Camel.

"Oh, yes," said Gladly.

"Which do you like better," said O Camel, "enjoying something to the full or to the empty?"

"I don't know," said Gladly.

"If you enjoy something to the empty," said O Camel, "you get more."

"That's true," said Gladly, uncertainly.

"So you aren't enjoying this to the full," said O Camel.

"So I'm not," said Gladly. "Good. Now we can go."

"These devices are good for jostling," said O Camel to himself with satisfaction, "so why should they be expected to hold water?"

They returned to the crossroads.

231

This time, Lady Mondegreen's counting-out rhyme came out like this:

> Waste sea, shine blue,
> Two barrels, wasted two,
> Dance through,
> One,
> Out.

And she pointed to TO THE BARREN WASTE.

"In spite of those barrels, which don't belong, this has a certain inevitability," said O Camel, wearily.

"It seems unlikely the Earl Amurray would be in a waste," said Lady Mondegreen."

"Let's wait until he comes out," said Gladly.

"He may be going in the other direction," said Lady Mondegreen. Off they started again.

This time the road wended and turned and wended and twisted between high hedges on either side. They were beginning to wonder when they would come to the barren waste, when the hedges abruptly stopped and they entered a small formal garden with a path leading to a stone bench at the other end. Seated on the bench was a tall thin distinguished gentleman with thin black hair, a long thin face, and a long thin nose. He wore a black doublet and hose.

"The Earl Amurray!" said Gladly. "Is it?"

Lady Mondegreen stopped at the beginning of the path and looked carefully at the thin gentleman.

"No," she said. "I don't know who it is, but it's not the Earl Amurray."

The gentleman got up and bowed politely.

"The Baron Waste," he said. "At your service. Be seated," and he indicated some iron chairs standing around on the grass.

They all sat down solemnly.

"How do you do," said Lady Mondegreen. "Have you seen the Earl Amurray?"

"Not well, not well at all," said the Baron Waste. "My despair is bad today. You would not believe, you could not conceive what I suffer."

"I'm sorry," said Lady Mondegreen. "Are you taking anything for it?"

"Everyone asks that," said the Baron, "as if it were an ordinary stomach-ache. It's especially special, especially extreme. None of the usual remedies work."

"What about fancy bread?" said O Camel.

"Couldn't be worse," said the Baron. "Aggravates the acid condition. Fancy bread is only good for children."

"Have you tried liver tea?" asked Lady Mondegreen. "Good Mrs. Murphy says it is good for everything that ails you."

"No, no," said the Baron Waste, wrinkling his nose with distaste. "The taste is too unspeakable, reekable." He closed his eyes and pressed his hand to his stomach. "Hollow, hollow," he moaned. "Doomed to remain so. Unhappy Baron!"

None of the friends could think of anything else to suggest. After a pause, the Baron Waste opened his eyes, sat up straight on the bench, and smiled resignedly.

"Even in a condition as absorbing as mine," he said, "one must observe the amenities. One must make the effort. People expect it, not thinking, not inkling of what's going on inside. You were asking about Amurray, Madam?"

"I am looking for him," said Lady Mondegreen.

"You'll be disappointed," said the Baron. "Oh, I've no

doubt you'll find him. He's all over the place. But he has gone off sadly, poor fellow, since we were younger."

Lady Mondegreen thought this over. "Where has he gone off sadly to?" she asked.

"Everywhere but here," said the Baron. "He never comes to see me any more. I don't blame him. I'm no entertainment, attainment, for someone like him. And I find him trying—the constant activity, the inevitable gallantry, the relentless brawness."

"Is the Earl Amurray a mondegreen?" asked Round John Virgin.

"I doubt it, old chap," said the Baron. "He's relatively grown up, in his way. A mondegreen is a maze, or a scape—childish, you know."

"I don't wish to contradict you," said Lady Mondegreen stiffly, "but the Earl Amurray *is* a mondegreen."

"If you know him better than I do, Madam," said the Baron, "there is nothing further to be said. Everyone has to learn by butter experience. That started my trouble. Butter does not agree with me."

"I don't believe I do," said Lady Mondegreen. "Butter was glowing under my chin before I ever tasted it."

"Amurray is a very sick person," said the Baron. "He doesn't realize it, of course."

"If he is, I will make him well," said Lady Mondegreen.

"I should be the last to wish to shake such supreme, such extreme confidence," said the Baron with dignity. "No matter how foolish, no matter how mulish!" he shouted.

"Why do you say things twice?" asked Round John Virgin.

"Once for me, and once for you not listening," groaned

the Baron. He clutched his stomach again. "This is bad for me," he said pathetically.

"Why don't you come with us?" said Lady Mondegreen. "A walk might do you good.

"Kind of you," said the Baron, "but you've aggravated me once. Even if you tried, I'd be expecting you to do it again. And I can't do without twice. I need it."

So they said good-by and started back to the crossroads.

As soon as they were out of hearing, Round John Virgin began to object. "We shouldn't have left so quickly," he said. "He's the only one so far who knew anything. I could have found out things to think about."

"I like rumination too," said O Camel, "but I was beginning to feel queasy. Every quest should leave questions unrequested."

Round John Virgin walked along trying things out to himself: "A mondegreen is a motion escaping. A mondegreen is amazed to stray," until they reached the crossroads.

Even though there was only one road left, Lady Mondegreen insisted on counting out again, because she had another rhyme in her head. It went like this:

> China blue, one barrel,
> Sea to sea to see Harold,
> Dance to no doubt,
> Ruled
> Out.

The minute she had said it, she opened her eyes in surprise.

"It's Harold we're going to see," she said triumphantly. "Of course. He'll know where the Earl Amurray is."

"Harold is exactly who I want to see," said Gladly.

"I should have guessed when that barrel sneaked in," said O Camel, "but it would have been more convenient if we had known it before."

"It didn't tell me before," said Lady Mondegreen. "Harold will give us a delicious tea."

"Liver?" said O Camel, suspiciously.

"Much more likely fancy bread," said Lady Mondegreen.

"To the China Sea," shouted Round John Virgin, and they started off down the fourth path.

It was lined on either side with ginkgo trees, and was the shortest path yet, for almost immediately they arrived. The China Sea was quite round and entirely blue and white. Along the edge were intricately gabled little Oriental houses, and on the opposite side and a little to the left was a small island, with a house partly concealed in bushes.

"There is Harold's house," said Lady Mondegreen. "The question is, how to get there."

As she spoke, a little boat with a square sail appeared in the middle of the sea, and began to sail toward them. Shipping its mast it floated under the bridge in front of them and rode up on the shore where they were standing. Out of it stepped a Chinese with a long pigtail, who bowed politely.

"My name is Lee Jun," he said.

They all bowed and said their names. When he heard Round John Virgin's, Lee Jun smiled broadly.

"Delighted to meet you," he said, "We must be cousins."

"Are we?" asked Round John Virgin, looking somewhat puzzled.

"Didn't you say your name was Ver Jun?" said Lee Jun. "I'm pleased to hear it. We'd lost track of the Ver branch."

"So it is," said Round John Ver Jun. "It's very nice to meet someone in the family. Are you a mondegreen?"

"I believe so," said Lee Jun. "A mondegreen is a go, and so is my boat."

"We would like to go across to Harold's house," said Lady Mondegreen. "How is Harold?"

"Full of the old nick," said Lee Jun. "He spent the morning trampling out the vintage where the grapes and rats are stored. It made him very angry, and he kept shouting 'Deliver us from weevils.' "

"Four heavens!" said O Camel. (This is a Tizzathee exclamation.) "We must think this over. Is this the best moment to see him? What is Harold like?"

"Harold is like everything and nothing," said Lee Jun. "Both at once and twice on Choosedays. It's better just to go."

"Very well," said O Camel. "I can think on and by the way."

"My boat, of course, is slow," said Lee Jun, "and Harold would like to get there faster. He likes company." He contemplated the boat, made several mysterious passes in the air, and said, "Thou whose word cannot be broken formed thee for his motor boat."

In a flash, the sailboat turned into a blue and white cabin cruiser with gleaming brass fittings.

Lee Jun motioned them all to climb in. They sat down on some blue-and-white striped cushions, and he disappeared below. There was a silence, then some banging, and then they heard him say "Drat!" Presently the motor started, and he appeared again.

"Machinery is new to me," he said as he sat down behind the wheel. "I am afraid it is something to think about."

The boat shot off over the white water. Lee Jun was not accustomed to so much speed, and turned the wheel frantically this way and that. The result was that they swooped back and forth, coming dangerously close to blue rocks and just missing willow trees which dripped into the water. It was nerve-racking, but they arrived at the small island without mishap.

They stepped ashore at the foot of a path, which led up to the house. Lee Jun waved good-by, and sailed off, for his boat immediately became a sailboat again.

When he was gone, they rushed up the path and arrived pall-mall in front of the house door, which was richly carved and closed. On the sill sat a large bird, purposefully, as if on a nest.

"Good afternoon," said Lady Mondegreen. "May we see Harold?"

"Let us observe the forms," said the bird. "First you look at me in surprise. Then you ask, curiously but courteously, 'What kind of bird are you?' "

"I know what you are," said Lady Mondegreen. "You're a dorkey bird."

The dorkey bird let out a squawk. "You've spoiled everything," it said. "I must have ceremony. Otherwise I have to ruffle my feathers, and I hate it."

"I beg your pardon," said Lady Mondegreen. "I wanted to speed things up. You don't have to ruffle your feathers."

"Just as much as you have to speed things up," said the bird. "It's a question of crowding. If we weren't crowded, you could be as unceremonious as you wished. But you need ceremony as much as I do. I could easily get us all called dorkeys, and then where would you be?"

"Right here," said Lady Mondegreen, who saw that this worked both ways. "You are."

"Exactly," said the bird. "So let us observe the forms."

"What is a dorkey?" asked Round John Ver Jun.

"A dorkey is a frontery," said the bird.

"Why not a backery?" asked Round John Ver Jun.

"I am in front," said the dorkey bird, "and you interrupted me. The point is"—it began to talk in a rich, public voice—"the golden real. Real unto other as you would have them real unto you. Often called the golden mean. The opposite of the golden mean is the undistributed middle, which is how you are behaving. Distribute and let's get this over with."

Lady Mondegreen blushed. She had been thinking that the dorkey bird did not need as much room as she did. "What would you rather be than?" she said dutifully.

The dorkey bird immediately smoothed down, and its feathers gleamed with bright colors like stained glass.

"I would rather be a dorkey bird in the house of my God," it said with satisfaction, "than dwell in the tents of wickedness. There."

But it had underestimated the crowding.

"What tense is wickedness?" asked Round John Ver Jun, settling down for a leisurely informative discussion. "Present inordinate," said the dorkey bird, wearily. "Don't remind me. I had to ruffle my feathers the whole time because of the cold. The tents of wickedness are a den of ice. I am happy in Harold's house, because it has a nice distributed warmth, smelling of cinnamon-flavored fancy bread."

"Cinnamon-flavored?" said Gladly. "We've never had that."

"Does Harold make it?" asked O Camel, and he looked more cheerful.

"Only occasionally,' said the bird. "Good Mrs. Murphy usually makes it."

"How did she get here?" asked Lady Mondegreen in surprise.

"She comes in by the day, which is more direct than your route," said the bird. "Who do you suppose does the washing, irons the angels' robes, and all those little chores? Good Mrs. Murphy is one of those who has entertained angels' underwears. Now I will let you in."

They all waited eagerly while the dorkey bird opened the door with its beak.

All but Lady Mondegreen, who hesitated on the steps and looked back. The China Sea had vanished, and all around Harold's house stretched a dim meadow, huge and indistinct, in which a human figure would have been a pin point. In the distance, the mizz blurred the limits of the meadow, and out of it, as if from a sea, rose high peaked mountains speaking of nothing except themselves. Lady Mondegreen shivered.

"It is a far world," she said, "and yet someone has walked on my grave."

"When I open the door," said the dorkey bird, tapping its claw, "you are to come in."

Lady Mondegreen turned and they all went into the house.

Inside was a large hall lined with columns. On the opposite side, Harold, looking very fit, sat on a gold throne. At his side stood Harkther, Harold's angel, tall, gaunt, and with straight yellow hair, in an Anglo-Saxon attitude. A number of small furry animals were chasing each other around the legs of the throne, and other angels and dark angels were coming and going in the hall. Spaced out around the walls were other thrones, all different. Some were grand; some simple; and one was a small tufted loveseat.

"Company. How nice," said Harold, clapping his hands. "How do you do?"

They bowed and Harold got up and came down from the throne, stumbling over one of the small animals, which promptly rolled up and lay still, playing dead.

"The twelve opossums *will* get under foot," said Harold. "But if one lives here, one becomes fond of them."

He shook hands with the four friends. "A pleasure to see you," he said. "Tea first. Questions later." He waved his hand and a large round table popped up through the floor in front of the throne. Chairs jumped into place around it. Harold clapped his hands and through a door in the back of the hall shot a familiar figure. It was Good Mrs. Murphy wearing a large pair of wings. She flew down the hall holding a laden tray in front of her and hovered over the table, lifting dishes and plates from the tray onto it.

"Don't forget the raisins, Good Mrs. Murphy," said Harold.

"Now, Mr. Harold," said Good Mrs. Murphy, hovering busily, "You can leave everything to spry old Good Mrs. Murphy. I hope you've all been behaving yourselves," she said to the friends. "No time to gossip," and she flew out again.

Harold sat down and surveyed the table with satisfaction. "Sit down, sit down," he said. "Pull your chairs in. Get as near me as you can, e'en though it be across that raisin tea."

The raisins, heaped up on a large platter, were a special kind, home-dried by Harold from the grapes he had driven the rats out of. There were many other things as well. Each of the friends immediately recognized something he knew he would particularly like.

"With the jellied toast proclaim," said O Camel, as he helped himself to some.

"Confirm the tidings—jelly roll!" said Gladly, happily.

Round John Ver Jun was stuffing himself on the raisins.

"There are libertine cheeses for all," said Harold, passing around a plate with several different kinds.

Lady Mondegreen paused. "I thought it was liver tea and just is," she said.

"A matter of emph," said Harold. "Emph as is or emph as isn't. Which would you rather have—a communion of saints or a union of snakes? You may take your choice, and there's something to be said for both."

"But which is the truth?" asked Round John Ver Jun.

"The truth is notonous," said Harold. "The opposite of monotonous, which, of course, is the most interesting thing there is."

"Have we had fancy bread?" asked O Camel, looking around the table, where by now absolutely everything had been eaten.

"Several kinds," said Harold. "Not all."

"What a tea! What a day!" said Gladly. "Is it Christmas?"

"Of course," said Harold. "Later on I will give you your presents. But first we should have some music, because you must come before his presents with a song. Or have you had too much to eat?"

"Not at all," said Lady Mondegreen. "We can sing, full though we be."

They all burst into song, and Harkther accompanied them skillfully on the A string from on high, which he pulled down, tucked under his chin, and stroked with a bow.

When the song was finished, they sat back, a little out of breath.

"Come from the dining room and blow," said Harold. "It's good for you after a big meal."

They got up from the table, which promptly vanished, and Harold lead them to the part of the hall where his throne was the tufted love seat, and where there were other comfortable chairs and couches. They all blew and sat down to relax.

"One of my more comfortable thrones," said Harold. He sat sideways in the love seat and put up his feet. "I'll start with you," and he pointed to Gladly. "What would you like?"

Gladly thought and his eyes crossed even further. "I would like what everyone else would like," he said.

"You want something that likes you," said Harold. He snapped his fingers, and at Gladly's side appeared another bear, also cinnamon-colored, but smaller.

"This is the child she-bear," he said. "She is too young to talk very much as yet, but she will learn." He pointed his finger at her. "Try something," he said.

"Gladly," said the child she-bear in a new voice.

"Good," said Harold. "What do you think you would like to do?"

"Pity mice implicitly," she said.

"Very good," said Harold. "For next week, memorize the 'Conquered Hen.' Everyone from Tizzathee should be able to do so."

"Thank you very much," said Gladly.

"No trouble," said Harold. "You're easy. All accept needs is to be accepted." He turned to O Camel.

"I would like something that would pay attention to what I say," said O Camel. "Being faithful is a burden, and I want some satisfaction out of it."

"Much better to have something whose attention you

243

can demand," said Harold. "It feels more important." He snapped his fingers again, and beside O Camel stood a small Arab boy in a burnoose. "This is Little Sedorum," said Harold.

Little Sedorum looked around the hall. "I shall pull the opussums' tails," he said, and he started off.

"O come, little Sedorum," said O Camel impatiently. Little Sedorum promptly came back. O Camel snorted happily.

"Thank you," he said. "That's extremely satisfactory."

"Now you," said Harold to Round John Ver Jun.

"I want answers," he said. "What is a mondegreen? What is the opposite of Christmas? Who am I?"

"Your father was Long John Silver," said Harold, "and your mother—let me think—Rounda Bout was her name. There has been some confusion about yours, hasn't there? We'll change it. From now on you will be Round John Verging. A mondegreen is in layers. That's all I'm going to tell you because I'm going to give you something to ask you questions. You'll like that better—there'll be twice as many answers."

For the third time he snapped his fingers and an odd animal appeared beside Round John Verging. It was a lion, or, to be exact, two halves of two lions. It had two legs and a head on each end, and where it came together in the middle it had two tails, one on either side. Occasionally they got tangled with each other.

"Do you come in layers?" asked Round John Verging.

"Do you?" asked one head. "Ask only what you're prepared to answer," said the other.

Round John Verging looked himself over. "Yes," he said.

"Layers as in cake?" asked one head. "Or lairs as in cave?" asked the other.

"Are you the cave kind?" asked Round John Verging.

"We're asking the questions," said the first head. "Define lairs in layers," said the other.

Round John Verging looked at Harold. "This is hard," he said.

"Talk back," said Harold.

"Turna Bout is fair play, in addition to being my first cousin," said Round John Verging to the heads. "I can ask you two questions, if I answer one."

The heads held a consultation. "Fair enough," they said, when they came out of their huddle.

"What are you for?" said Round John Verging.

"That's four questions," said the heads.

"Who are you?" he amended.

"Reverse Noel," said one head. "Leon," said the other. "Now it's our turn."

"No, it isn't," said Round John Verging. "I've only asked one."

"You got two answers," said one head. "You must have asked two questions," said the other. "Our turn," they said firmly in unison.

"All right," said Round John Verging.

"What's reverse Noel?" they asked.

"The opposite of Christmas," said Round John Verging.

"I would like to submit, sir," said the first head to Harold, "that that is a tautology," said the second, "and doesn't count."

"Out of sleight, out of hand," said Harold. "You've been a little tautological yourselves. He has to be taught a logic, but you have to take the consequences."

"My turn," said Round John Verging. "Why do you have two heads?"

"To give you two answers," they said.

"What is a mondegreen?" said Round John Verging quickly, before they could say that he had asked two questions.

"A mondegreen is a vocative," said one head, gaily. "A mondegreen is a pityme," said the other, sadly.

"Please, sir," said Round John Verging to Harold, "Those aren't the same thing."

"They both call," said one head. "How much correspondence must he have?" said the other.

"You're all correct," said Harold, "but you mustn't keep coming to me for help. You must learn to fight in the corner where you are."

"Just one question," said Round John Verging.

"Very well," said Harold.

"What is this?" asked Round John Verging.

"Reverse Noel is three hundred and sixty-four days of the year," said Harold, "as you should know. Which, as you not necessarily should know, is the life of elastic. That's enough for the present." He looked around.

"Ah, yes," he said, as his eye fell on Lady Mondegreen. "What do you think?"

"You made me up, and you made me up right," said Lady Mondegreen. "But I am left. You cannot give me the Earl Amurray."

"Very good," said Harold. "Now I will ask you a riddle. Why is Amurray like the measles?"

"Because I will come down with him," said Lady Mondegreen.

"All around my house," said Harold, "is a green world

with many green paths, some for the euphoric and some for the you're-for-it, some for the weary and some for the wearisome, some for the fortunate and some for the too late. There is even a path for Punches Pilate, and there is also a path for a bunch of violets. As far as you can be and as near as you can see, as far away as you can think and as here as you can blink stretches the green world. In it is your castle, and the Earl Amurray gallops the paths. Your friends will take you there."

Lady Mondegreen stopped in the kitchen to say good-by to Good Mrs. Murphy, who refused to, saying, "You should know by now that you haven't seen the last of tough old Good Mrs. Murphy."

After that, Harold saw them off, standing in the door of his house with his hand resting on the dorkey bird's head. Leon led the way, with Lady Mondegreen riding on his back with the two tails wrapped around her to hold her in place. Behind him came the child she-bear and Little Sedorum. Round John Verging, O Camel, and Gladly brought up the rear, conversing together like veterans.

Far in the distance of the green world gleamed the crenelated battlements of the castle, and the banner over it said AMURRAY.

Harold waved as long as Lady Mondegreen, looking over her shoulder, could see him.

"What time is it?" asked the dorkey bird, when they had finally faded from sight.

"It's wit's-end tide," said Harold. "I am going to take a nap."

He went indoors. The dorkey bird settled down again on the sill to wait for the next thing.

END

ABOUT THE AUTHOR

Sylvia Wright's first substantial work was a verse play about the nine muses, written when she was nine. But, as is true of many American writers, this early burst of promise was followed by a run-of-the-mill, middle-twentieth-century literary career. She worked in publishing (Farrar & Rinehart), for the Office of War Information in New York and overseas, for the magazine *Harper's Bazaar*, and for the OWI's peacetime successor, the U.S. Information Service. She cut and edited for publication her father, Austin Wright's, long novel, *Islandia*, and has herself been published in such typical middle-twentieth-century magazines as *Harper's*, *Harper's Bazaar*, *Vogue*, *The Reporter*, and *High Fidelity*.

After a search of the available biographical material, it can be said that Sylvia Wright is unquestionably the only American writer with twenty-five ribs who has contributed to all three of the following publications: the Buckingham School (Cambridge, Mass.) *Packet*, the Bryn Mawr College *Lantern*, and *Glas Pobede*. Only the invidious would attempt to discount the last-named on the bases that any contribution of Miss Wright's was lost in translation into Serbo-Croat, and that a good many copies of *Glas Pobede*, a very little magazine, were certainly lost in the forests of Yugoslavia, when dropped there by air during the last part of World War II. How these diverse influences ever came together to create the present book is still unexplained. It is to be doubted if it will ever be clear to anyone, including, fortunately, Miss Wright.